ST. LOUIS
DE MONTFORT

ST. LOUIS DE MONTFORT

THE STORY OF OUR LADY'S SLAVE, ST. LOUIS MARY GRIGNION DE MONTFORT

By
Mary Fabyan Windeatt

Illustrated by
Paul A. Grout

TAN Books
An Imprint of Saint Benedict Press, LLC
Charlotte, North Carolina

Nihil Obstat: Francis J. Reine, S.T.D.
      Censor Librorum

Imprimatur: ✠ Paul C. Schulte, D.D.
      Archbishop of Indianapolis
      November 16, 1957

ISBN: 978-0-89555-414-7

Library of Congress Catalog Card No.: 90-71826

Printed and bound in the United States of America.

TAN Books
An Imprint of Saint Benedict Press, LLC
Charlotte, North Carolina
2013

For
His Excellency
the Most Reverend
Joseph E. Ritter, S.T.D.,
Archbishop of St. Louis,
who as seminarian and later as Archbishop
made pilgrimages
to the shrine of Our Lady
on the hill
where this book was written.

ACKNOWLEDGMENTS

The author wishes to thank the Dominican Fathers of the Dominican House of Studies, River Forest, Illinois, for the use of much valuable source material concerning the life and times of Saint Louis Mary Grignion De Montfort. Also the Montfort Fathers of Saint Louis De Montfort Seminary, Litchfield, Connecticut, and of the Montfort Preparatory Seminary, Bay Shore, New York, for their helpful comments and suggestions regarding this little story—a dramatic account of the life and work of their holy founder.

CONTENTS

ST. LOUIS
DE MONTFORT

CHAPTER 1

A FOOL OR A SAINT?

THE Bishop of Poitiers peered through his study window at the shabbily dressed young priest striding briskly toward the front gate in the pale sunlight of the late November afternoon. Then, shivering at the whistle of the chill wind through the leafless trees, he turned, and, leaning heavily on a cane, moved toward the open hearth where a fire was burning.

"Father Louis Mary Grignion," he muttered wearily, shaking his head as he warmed himself over the leaping flames. "That young man is either a fool or a saint."

For several minutes the Bishop gazed moodily into the fire, heedless of the fact that there had been a knock at the door and that now his secretary stood waiting in respectful silence on the threshold. Then slowly he came to himself.

"Yes, Monsignor? What is it?"

The newcomer, a tall, severe-looking man in his middle forties, bowed stiffly. "I brought the papers, Your Lordship. The ones you wanted about Father Grignion. But shall we go over them now? After all, it's nearly supper time. . . . "

The Bishop hesitated, then hobbled painfully across the room to his desk. "Of course we'll go over them now. Father Grignion's case is most important. Besides, it'll take only a few minutes."

1

The Monsignor bowed again, then placed a sheaf of papers before his superior.

"Very well, Your Lordship. But I'm afraid you'll find everything as it was last month. For instance, on this first page is the personal information about Father Grignion. Birth: January 31, 1673, at Montfort-la-Cane, in Brittany, the second of eighteen children of John Baptist Grignion and Joan Robert. Education: seven years at the Jesuit college in Rennes, seven years with the Sulpicians in Paris. Ordination to the holy priesthood last year on June 5, 1700, aged twenty-seven. After that, a few retreats and missions under Father Lévêque at Nantes. . . . "

The Bishop listened in moody silence. Then suddenly he shifted impatiently. "Yes, yes, Monsignor. I know all this. But the letters from his former superiors in Paris. Surely there are some new ones by now? What have they to say? That's what I want to hear."

The Monsignor smiled wryly. "There's been nothing new, Your Lordship."

"Not even from Father Leschassier? Or Father Brenier? Or Father de la Chétardie?"

"No, Your Lordship. None of these men will recommend Father Grignion for any work—let alone what you've just given him to do here in Poitiers at the poorhouse."

A hard light shone in the Bishop's eyes. "But what have they got against the boy?" he demanded sharply. "Hasn't he always been at the top of his classes in the Seminary? Hasn't he even had to do outside work to pay his tuition? Hasn't he been prayerful, mortified, obedient, all through his student years?"

"Yes, Your Lordship."

"Well, go on. What is it, then?"

"His . . . his professors say he's too different, Your Lordship."

"Different! How different?"

"Well, for one thing, his clothes. He just doesn't seem to care what they look like, Your Lordship. Why, he won't even wear a hat!"

The Bishop shrugged. "A hat! What has wearing a hat got to do with being a good priest?"

"Nothing, Your Lordship. But still, when all other priests wear hats. . . . "

"Go on. What else is wrong with Father Grignion?"

The Monsignor hesitated. He had no wish to become involved in an argument with the Bishop. But he could not help feeling slightly suspicious of the young priest (at present a missionary in Nantes), who only a few minutes before had been in this very room. Not only had his clothes been disgracefully shabby; he had not even seemed to care that they were. Nor had he been a bit impressed with all the elegance around him—the rich carpets, the hangings, the furniture. The approaching interview with the Bishop seemed to have produced in him none of the anxiety which the Monsignor ordinarily observed in other visitors.

Even more. When the time came, he had found Father Louis Mary Grignion, not sitting timidly in a chair, or pacing nervously about the waiting room, but on his knees in prayer. And here he had received the Monsignor's announcement that the Bishop awaited him quite simply, without apology or sign of embarrassment.

"Well, Monsignor? As you were saying. . . ?"

The latter swallowed hard. "Really, Your Lordship, I haven't a thing against Father Grignion. I'm sure that he's very holy. And that he'll do good work at the poorhouse."

Gradually the Bishop's eyes softened. "I'm glad to hear you say that. The place is in a dreadful state." Then, after a moment: "But you really don't think he'll stay, do you?"

"Frankly, no, Your Lordship."

"Why not?"

The Monsignor felt slightly suspicious.

With a gesture of despair, the Monsignor threw caution to the winds. "Because he's not prudent! He's bound to make enemies among the staff! Mark my words, this very night he'll be preaching a sermon on the Blessed Virgin and trying to get members for that society of his!"

"*Society?*"

"Yes, the one that's mentioned here in these papers. He began it when he was only a student at the Seminary. And what an unfortunate title he chose—'The Slaves of Mary'!"

"The Slaves of Jesus *in* Mary," corrected the Bishop.

"Very well. Even so, the word 'slaves' is repulsive, Your Lordship. It has nothing to do with holiness. Why, such a group could do real harm to the Church!"

The Bishop nodded thoughtfully. "Yes, if it were misunderstood. But let's hope that doesn't happen here in Poitiers, Monsignor. In fact, let's pray that Father Grignion's work at the poorhouse will be blessed with real success."

Quickly remorseful over his outburst, the Monsignor smiled awkwardly. "Well, of course that would be the charitable thing to do. But on the other hand. . . ."

"Good. After all, who knows? Perhaps someday our only claim to God's mercy will be that we helped one of His chosen workers through a difficult time. Now," with a gesture toward the papers scattered on his desk, "since it's after five o'clock. . . ."

With a feeling of genuine relief the Monsignor hastily collected the papers, then helped the Bishop to his feet. What a difficult afternoon this had been! And what a blessing that it was almost time for supper!

CHAPTER 2

A SLAVE

AS Father Louis Mary Grignion strode through the streets of Poitiers, the Bishop's encouraging words still ringing in his ears, his heart sang. What a wonderful day this was! He, twenty-eight years old, with only a few months experience as a missionary in Nantes, was going to live and work among the poor in the city—and at their own request!

"It's almost too good to be true," he told himself happily.

And yet how very true it was! Six months earlier, after visiting his sister Sylvia at the Benedictine convent of Fontevrault, he had come to Poitiers to see the Bishop about the possibility of working in his diocese. But the Bishop had been away at the time, and having nowhere else to stay while awaiting his return, he had gone to the General Hospital (commonly known as the poorhouse) to ask for bed and board.

Now, as he recalled that far-off day in early May, Father Grignion's eyes twinkled. Because of the shabby cloak which had enveloped him, few at the poorhouse had taken him to be a priest. They had thought him just another beggar, and had accommodated him accordingly. But when his true identity had become known, and better quarters immediately found for him, he had politely declined them,

6

preferring to be among the poorest of the lodgers.

God had blessed this decision. The influence of the strange young priest from Nantes rapidly showed itself at the poorhouse. Men and women who had not been to church in years assisted at his Mass each morning and even joined with him three times a day in reciting the Rosary. When it was time for Father Grignion to return to Nantes (for the Bishop had been unable to find a place for him in the diocese), the poor themselves had come to his aid by taking up a collection for him. They had then petitioned the Bishop to let him be their chaplain. Even the staff had been most anxious that he remain.

"And now His Lordship's finally agreed to everything," Father Grignion reflected gratefully. "God be praised!"

But if Father Grignion was happy over the recent turn of events, others in Poitiers were even more so. And when, amid the fast-gathering shadows of the November twilight he presently arrived at the front gate of the poorhouse, a sizeable crowd had collected in the chilly courtyard to bid him welcome. Others—the lame and feeble—peered eagerly from the windows. Even the blind and bedridden heard the news with fresh hope. Father Grignion was back! How different life was going to be from now on!

"Father, we thought you'd never get here!"

"Oh, Father! Remember me?"

"And me?"

"Look, Father! My arm got better—just as you said it would when you were here in May!"

"And my foot! It got better, too, right after you blessed it!"

"Hurry, Father! Supper's ready! A very special one in your honor!"

As he gazed at the excited men and women crowding about him in the windswept courtyard, garbed in the drab grey homespun of the poorhouse, their faces pinched and wan yet shining with childlike eagerness, a lump came into

Father Grignion's throat. Souls! The souls of the poor and unwanted! What a privilege to be their friend!

"I must do everything to help them," he thought, as he let himself be pulled along toward the front door. "Dear Blessed Mother, you *will* show me how, won't you?"

There was little time for prayer now, however. Not only was supper ready and waiting. The matron was anxious to show Father Grignion the room which had been prepared for him, to hear all about what had happened since his first visit in May and to learn what plans he had for the future.

But when supper was over and Father Grignion had visited the blind and bedridden and made the acquaintance of several newcomers, a sudden thought came to him. The poor would soon be retiring for the night, but surely it was not too late to have a meeting with the staff?

At this unexpected suggestion, the matron hesitated. Darkness came on early in November. And since it was cold and damp in the house because of the shortage of fuel. . . .

Father Grignion smiled understandingly. "Don't worry. I won't keep you long."

"But you must be so tired, Father!"

"No, no. Please, couldn't you arrange to get your helpers together for just a little while?"

"Well, of course, Father. If you really want it that way. . . ."

So presently, in a large and rather cheerless room, Father Grignion found himself facing the matron, her assistants, the staff of nurses, maids and kitchen workers. A number of men in charge of various duties around the house were also on hand. All looked at him expectantly.

For a moment a doubt crossed Father Grignion's mind. Perhaps it hadn't been the wisest thing to call these men and women together so soon after his arrival, especially since they must have worked hard all day. Certainly this was now their free time, and no doubt some of them had made plans of their own. But his heart was so full! He wanted everyone to know how much he appreciated being back in Poitiers, and of all the things he hoped to do to make the poorhouse into a real home.

"Friends, I know the city doesn't allow much money for the work here," he began. "I understand about the shortage of fuel, even of food at certain times. And I know you're paid very little for all your labors. But—well, I think there'll be changes before long."

Then, to the astonishment of everyone present, he announced that in the morning he was going out to beg. There were plenty of rich people in Poitiers. When they heard of the urgent needs at the poorhouse, surely they would not refuse him.

"To beg! Ah, I see that this shocks you," said Father Grignion, smiling, "that some of you don't like the idea at all. But friends, didn't you know? *I'm* a *slave!* The slave of Jesus, in Mary! And right now, begging for others is the work I've been given to do."

There was a gasp of astonishment, but Father Grignion, eyes sparkling with enthusiasm, paid little heed. Why shouldn't his co-workers know the truth about him? That years ago, while still only a student in the Seminary of Saint Sulpice in Paris, he had offered himself, body and soul, to the Blessed Virgin for her to do with as she would? That he had kept back nothing—not even the satisfactory merit of his prayers and good works—so that she herself might apply these to whatever needy souls she wished to help?

"Yes, I'm a slave," he continued, smiling at the startled faces raised to his. "The slave of Jesus, in Mary. Oh, if I just had words to tell you what this really means. . . . "

CHAPTER 3

TROUBLE WITH THE POORHOUSE STAFF

FATHER Grignion's confidence was quickly rewarded, and his zeal and devotion became known throughout the city. Scores of people, formerly indifferent to the plight of the poor, began to see what they could do to help. Thus, when he made his daily begging rounds through the streets, leading a sturdy donkey with two ample bags hanging from its sides, young and old came hurrying out with what they could spare of food, clothing, money and other gifts.

"God be praised for sending Father Grignion to us!" was the heartfelt prayer of the four hundred men and women living at the poorhouse. "We've never had such attention before."

"Why, now there's even enough to eat for everyone!" "And the whole house has been cleaned from top to bottom!"

"And painted, too!"

"Yes. And the chapel! Have you ever seen anything more beautiful?"

As the weeks passed, however, Father Grignion was forced to admit that in his zeal for the welfare of the poor he was making enemies as well as friends, particularly among the staff. The matron especially was none too pleased with his methods.

"You're really pampering the people here, Father," she

10

"Thank God for Father Grignion!"

announced indignantly one day. "Meat for dinner two and three times a week! As many blankets as each person wants! The rooms to be dusted every morning! New curtains at the windows! The floors to be *scrubbed,* as well as swept! Really, Father, it's too much. The poor maids are beginning to complain."

With difficulty Father Grignion restrained the impatient words which sprang to his lips. The poor maids! Even when he had been but a visitor here in Poitiers, he had noticed that the maids were a shiftless lot. They did no more work than was absolutely required. In fact, a good many of them were downright heartless, and the nurses, too. They thought nothing of leaving the bedridden without attention for hours at a time.

"I'm sorry the maids are finding the work so hard," he said dryly.

At the tone in his voice, the matron hesitated. Until Father Grignion's arrival, she and her assistants had managed affairs at the poorhouse pretty much as they had wished. With the money allotted to them, they had bought food and clothing, hired help, paid the bills and otherwise seen to details. But now, by order of the Bishop, all these duties were in Father Grignion's hands. He was the superior, and no one else had any real authority.

"Well?" smiled Father Grignion, seeming to read her thoughts. "Perhaps some people are sorry that I came?"

The smile and words were so unexpected that for a moment the matron—a shrewd woman—was taken off guard. Then she quickly recovered her composure. "Oh, no, Father. The . . . the poor themselves are very fond of you. It's just that. . . . "

"Go on. What else is wrong?"

"Well, the handymen say they have too much to do. There's not a day goes by but you want them to make repairs about the house."

"And why not? The place is terribly run down. And if the men are paid, why shouldn't they be glad to work?"

"But they've never put in such long hours before, Father! As for the nurses—well, they're all saying the same thing. You expect them to be servants for the poor wretches who come to us. And they don't like it, Father. They don't like it at all."

For a moment Father Grignion was silent, reminding himself that on no account must he lose patience with the matron, or with anyone else on the staff. After all, not every person had the grace to see Christ in the poor and sick. But, apart from that, on the very night of his arrival he had assured his co-workers that he knew they were paid very little for their labors, and that soon he hoped to remedy this.

"Suppose that today everyone here were to get a raise in salary," he suggested finally. "Do you think that would help?"

Suddenly the matron was all smiles and graciousness. "Oh, Father! What a splendid idea!"

"So—you do think that would help?"

"Oh, yes! Particularly when you can afford it." Father Grignion's eyes narrowed. *"Afford it?"*

"Yes. After all, everyone knows that you've taken in quite a lot of money since you came here."

For a moment Father Grignion said nothing. Then he nodded slowly. "Yes, the people of Poitiers have been most generous. But surely you realize that everything they give me is spent almost as soon as I get it? For instance, aren't the meals better these days? The house well-heated? Comfortable beds for the sick? New shoes and clothing, furniture, improvements in the chapel. . . ."

The matron shrugged. "Yes, Father. But many of us don't think all these things are necessary. For this *is* a poorhouse, isn't it? And since the people here have always got along with just a little, why spoil them now with luxuries?"

Once again Father Grignion had all he could do to control his impatience. "I guess we needn't worry about all this just now," he said quietly. "Instead, suppose you spread the word that there'll be a meeting of the staff this afternoon, at which time we'll talk about a raise in salary for everyone."

The matron smiled. "Very well, Father. I'll go and tell them right away."

The words were spoken pleasantly enough; nevertheless a cold chill settled over Father Grignion's heart as the door closed behind the matron. Could it be that this woman was turning against him? Why, only a few short weeks ago she had joined with everyone else at the poorhouse in begging the Bishop to put him in charge of the work! Now—

"I do believe the poor woman is jealous," he decided finally.

It was a depressing thought, but the more Father Grignion considered it, the more likely it seemed to be. Yes, the matron *was* jealous. When she had been in charge of the poorhouse, there had never been the funds to spare that were now on hand because of the daily begging trips through the city. Even more. The matron and her friends had no real love for the poor. They wanted any extra money spent on themselves. They could not bear to see it used for the four hundred wretched people in their charge.

"If only some nursing Sisters could be brought here to the poorhouse!" thought Father Grignion. "Women who would be glad to work for the afflicted because Christ Himself lives in them!"

But where were such women to be found? Despite the remarkable growth of the Daughters of Charity (founded in Paris by Father Vincent de Paul some sixty-nine years before), the Society was not as yet established in Poitiers. And since most of the other religious Orders for women were cloistered . . . .

Suddenly the harassed look faded from Father Grignion's eyes. What was the use of worrying? The work he was trying to do was God's work. If he prayed and did his best, everything would turn out well.

CHAPTER 4

FATHER GRIGNION DISAPPEARS

FOR the next few days all was peaceful at the poorhouse. Satisfied with the increase in their salaries, the matron and her assistants made no more complaints. Meals were nourishing, and served on time. The rooms were kept clean. Even the difficult cases among the sick were cared for properly.

"Maybe I was mistaken about the matron," Father Grignion ventured to tell himself one day. "Oh, how I hope so!"

But in March of the year 1702, when he had been at the poorhouse some four months, there came a terrible trial for Father Grignion. The Bishop of Poitiers fell ill and died! Of course he had been in poor health for many years, so that his death was no surprise to anyone. Still. . . .

"The Bishop was the first real friend I ever had here," Father Grignion reflected sadly. "Dear God, what am I going to do without him? Especially if things don't go well at the poorhouse?"

Yet after a while some measure of consolation filled the young priest's heart. Bishop Anthony Girard had loved the poor. From the beginning he had done what he could to make their lives more bearable. He had prayed and suffered for them, too, through the many years of his illness. Well, was God to be outdone in generosity? Surely, when he died, the Bishop had gone straight to Heaven and was now a saint?

"I'll ask him to help me," Father Grignion decided. "And not only with the work at the poorhouse, but with my other work, too."

Other work? Yes, by now Father Grignion had discovered that he could be of use to all the people of Poitiers, not just to those under his immediate care. And so at regular intervals he preached in various churches throughout the city, heard confessions, visited the needy and taught catechism to young and old alike.

"You really ought to go and hear him preach," Elizabeth Trichet told her young sister Mary Louise one day. "I don't think I've ever heard anyone speak so touchingly before about . . . well, about heavenly things."

Seventeen-year-old Mary Louise looked up in amazement. Elizabeth, devout enough in her own way, had certainly never been given to enjoying sermons, much less to remembering them.

"*You* went to hear Father Grignion?" she demanded incredulously.

"Yes. Last week, at the Church of Saint Austrégésilde. And listen, Mary Louise. Do you know who is everybody's best friend? Oh, I don't mean just the people living here in Poitiers, or even in France, but in England, in Germany, in Italy, in Africa, even in China and Japan. *Everywhere!*"

Puzzled, Mary Louise shook her head. "No. Who?"

"Why, the Blessed Virgin, of course! And if you want to be a saint without a lot of trouble, all you have to do is to ask her to help you, then do what she says."

Mary Louise could scarcely believe her ears. "Elizabeth! What a thing to say! As though you could talk to the Mother of God and have her talk to you! Why, it's not . . . well, *reverent* even to imagine such a thing!"

"And why not?"

"Because Our Lady is millions of miles away. I mean, she's in heaven, and she never committed a sin in her whole life. And . . . well, you just can't talk to her like you can to a real person. As for calling her your best friend. . . . "

"But you've got to do that, if you want to be a saint quickly. Father Grignion said so. Now, listen. Suppose you wanted to make a statue. How would you go about it?"

Mary Louise stared. Had Elizabeth taken leave of her senses?

"I haven't the least desire to make a statue," she said uncooperatively. "As for knowing how to go about it. . . . "

"Well, there are two ways you can make one. You can get some stone, and a hammer and chisel, and pound and cut on your statue. That's the hard way, because one slip of the tools and everything may be ruined. Besides, stone isn't easy to work with. And it's expensive, too. Or you can get a mold—one that a real artist has made—and pour in some soft material, like plaster or clay. When it hardens, you'll have a perfect statue with scarcely any trouble or expense."

Then, as Mary Louise continued to stare in silent amazement, Elizabeth went on eagerly to explain. The Blessed Virgin, according to Saint Augustine and Father Grignion, was "the living mold of God." Christ had been formed in her without losing any of the divine perfection of the Father or of the Holy Spirit. And a person who wanted to be as perfect as possible—that is, a saint, or another Christ—would do well to remember this.

"Father Grignion says it's foolish to try to make ourselves perfect just by our own efforts,* and even run the risk of failing, when Our Lady is so anxious to do the work for us," she declared emphatically.

"But . . . but I don't understand!"

*See Note on page 91.

"Didn't I just tell you about the mold? All we have to do is to give ourselves to the Blessed Virgin, and she'll make us into another Christ—*if we let her.* Oh, Mary Louise! You really ought to go and hear Father Grignion preach. He explains things ever so much better than I can!"

For the rest of the day, Mary Louise found herself pondering her sister's words. Yes, it would be good to hear one of Father Grignion's sermons. And since he seemed to be such a holy man, perhaps it would be well to go to confession to him, too, and ask his advice as to what she was going to do with her life. For she was so confused and unhappy! About a year ago she had spent some months in a convent of the Daughters of Notre Dame at Châtellerault, hoping that she might end her days there as a lay Sister. But her health had not been too good, and finally the superiors had decided that she had no vocation to the life and ought to return home. Ever since, how miserable she had been! How lost and forsaken!

"Yes, I'll go to confession to Father Grignion," she reflected. "I'll ask him what it is that God wants of me."

But a great disappointment was in store for Mary Louise, and for many others in Poitiers who had hoped to speak with Father Grignion. For without the slightest warning he had disappeared. Rumor had it that he had gone to make a retreat with the Jesuit Fathers, and would not be coming back.

"They say it's all the fault of that matron at the poorhouse! *And* her staff!" declared Elizabeth Trichet indignantly. "Despite all he's done for them, they've made things so unpleasant for Father Grignion that he just couldn't stand it any longer. Oh, what a shame!"

Mary Louise was almost in tears. "But . . . but what am I going to do?" she asked. "I just know he could have helped me. Now—"

Elizabeth hesitated. Undoubtedly Father Grignion could

have been of great use to Mary Louise. Perhaps he might even have been able to have her admitted to some other convent.

"Well, don't worry, dear," she said comfortingly. "Everything's going to turn out all right. And maybe one of these days . . . ."

"Y-yes?"

"God will do something about that wretched troublemaker at the poorhouse. And all her helpers, too."

CHAPTER 5

FATHER GRIGNION'S ADVICE

SOON Elizabeth's words came true. A strange illness (which many believed to be the plague) came upon the poorhouse. More than eighty men and women were stricken, including the matron and several of her friends.

"See? God's put a curse on the poorhouse," the residents of Poitiers told one another fearfully. "And maybe on the rest of the city, too, because of the shameful way Father Grignion was treated."

Of course everyone was filled with fear, especially when deaths began to occur at the poorhouse almost every day. Oh, if only Father Grignion could be brought back! If only there was some way to make up to him for all that he had suffered from evil and jealous tongues! Then, without announcement, Father Grignion did return. But to all questions concerning the rumor that he had left the poorhouse for good, he only smiled and shook his head. Quietly he took up his former duties—feeding the hungry, nursing the sick, comforting the dying, burying the dead. And without the slightest sign of fear, or a single word of reproach to anyone.

Still, death continued to claim its victims at the poorhouse, the matron and several of her co-workers among them. But after some weeks, people began to breathe more freely. The strange illness which had struck so suddenly and taken so many lives was definitely on the wane. Possibly, now that Father Grignion's chief enemies were gone. . . .

"Do you think he'll stay at the poorhouse?" was one of the questions on everyone's lips.

"Of course not. Why should he, after what he's suffered there?"

"But what's going to become of the place?"

"Who knows? Or cares?"

"But since the matron's dead. . . ."

"And a good many of the other troublemakers. . . ."

"That's right. Things mightn't be so hard for him now."

"Maybe if a petition were drawn up. . . ."

Finally Father Grignion put an end to all speculation. In November 1701, he explained, Bishop Anthony Girard had asked him to do what he could for the poor of the city. On the Bishop's death in March 1702, the authorities had begged him to remain. Therefore, he would certainly continue working at the poorhouse until the new Bishop, Claude de la Poype de Vertrieu, ordered otherwise. As for his recent disappearance, gossip had been partially true. He had gone to make a retreat with the Jesuit Fathers. But there had been no reason to say that he would not return.

"God be praised!" cried everyone thankfully. "Then things *are* all right!"

"Yes. Father Grignion's going to stay."

"He doesn't hold a grudge against anyone."

"No. He even offers Mass for the very people who persecuted him."

"And he won't listen to a harsh word against any of them —living or dead."

"Well, he must be a saint."

"Yes, he certainly must be."

Like so many others in Poitiers, Mary Louise Trichet rejoiced at the news of Father Grignion's return, and one day, after he had preached in one of the parish churches, she approached his confessional. But not without anxiety. For what was the best way to tell her story without taking up too much time? So many other people wanted to go to confession.

Scarcely had she knelt down in the confessional and begun to relate her problems, when Father Grignion interrupted.

"Child, who sent you to me?" he asked.

At the unusual question Mary Louise hesitated. "Why, my sister Elizabeth, Father. She heard you preach one day. And . . . and she told me to come."

For a moment Father Grignion made no reply. Then suddenly from out the darkness came his voice—startlingly intense and eager. "No, it wasn't your sister. It was the Blessed Virgin."

"The . . . *the Blessed Virgin,* Father?"

"Yes. She has a wonderful work in store for you. Did you know that?"

"N-no, Father. I just wanted to ask your advice. . . . "

"You love Our Lady, don't you?"

"Why, of course, Father."

"You say her Rosary every day?"

"Well . . . no. Not every day."

"But you must, child! You must! It's such an easy way to earn graces for yourself. Then, Our Lady's litany! Oh, if you knew how much she loves to be called by those beautiful names! *Cause of our Joy! Mystical Rose! Gate of Heaven! Health of the Sick!* Yes, from now on you must say Our Lady's litany every day, too, slowly and carefully. That will win even more graces for you and your work."

Mary Louise shifted uneasily. "Father, I don't know what you mean," she said respectfully. "I just came to ask

"Child, who sent you to me?"

your advice about entering the convent. You see, the Daughters of Notre Dame at Châtellerault don't think I have a vocation to their life. Still, I want to be a nun somewhere and I thought that . . . well, maybe you could tell me where to go."

In silence Father Grignion listened to the rest of Mary Louise's story. Then finally he spoke:

"Child, how old are you?"

"Seventeen, Father."

"Seventeen? Then you have lots of time to think about the future. For the present, just do what I've told you. Say Our Lady's Rosary every day, and her litany, too, then come back to see me in a week."

"But what about entering the convent, Father? I still don't know. . . . "

"Don't worry about the convent. You will be a nun some day, never fear. Right now, all you must think about is getting to know Our Lady better. For it's impossible to love a person we don't know anything about, isn't it?"

"Y-yes, Father, I guess so."

"Of course it is. Well, you must learn to know Our Lady—*really* know her—so that you can love her very much. Then you'll be able to do the work she has in store for you. And oh, child, what a glorious work it is! Why, it can mean the saving of thousands—yes, millions—of souls!"

CHAPTER 6

CONSECRATION TO MARY

AS the weeks passed, Mary Louise became more and more puzzled. Father Grignion was constantly referring to the work which Our Lady had in store for her, yet he never gave the slightest clue as to what it might be. Nor did he seem to be making any effort to have her enter the religious life.

"Don't worry. You will be a nun some day," he kept repeating.

But Mary Louise did worry. And not only about her own future, but about that of Father Grignion, too. For evil tongues were beginning to wag once more. It seemed that the new matron was just as selfish and jealous as the old one, and there was constant quarreling and misunderstanding. Often, because of her, Father Grignion's orders were not only disregarded by the nurses and other workers but ridiculed as well.

"There's going to be trouble again," Mary Louise told herself fearfully, "I just know it."

Father Grignion paid little attention to the lies and gossip about him, but naturally he was hurt when his orders were not carried out and distressed when the poor went hungry or were neglected. To the best of his ability he then undertook the tasks which others considered beneath them

26

—making beds, cleaning rooms, serving meals, tending the sick—often working far into the night before he could retire to his own quarters to pray and make plans for the future.

"There's just one joy for the poor man," an indignant Mary Louise told Elizabeth one day. "That's the Wisdom Group. They, at least, never cause him any trouble."

Elizabeth's eyes widened. "The Wisdom Group? Why, what in the world is that?" she asked curiously.

Mary Louise lost no time in explaining. A few days ago, at Father Grignion's request, she had paid a visit to the poorhouse and had met the various members of the Wisdom Group. And what an experience it had been! Never in all her seventeen years had she known the like.

"The Wisdom Group? Well, it's a number of women invalids at the poorhouse who are leading something of the religious life, Elizabeth. Some are lame, others deaf or deformed, and one—the superior—is totally blind. And all these good women live together in one big room."

"You mean they never go anywhere else?"

"Oh, yes. Those who can get about help Father Grignion with his various duties. But most of all the Wisdom Group prays, especially to Our Lady. And in the room where they live, Father Grignion has put a plain wooden cross— a big one. That's to remind the group of the reason for their existence."

"*A cross?* I don't entirely see the connection."

"Well, the cross—or suffering—*is* wisdom, Elizabeth. For only the wisest people, through a special gift of God, have the grace to understand it. Oh, you'll have to come and meet the Wisdom Group yourself! They'll really give you something to think about."

Elizabeth did accompany Mary Louise to the poorhouse, and was deeply impressed by the Wisdom Group. To think that some twenty poor cripples were offering their prayers and sufferings for sinners throughout the world! Even more. That, following Father Grignion's suggestion, they had consecrated themselves, body and soul, to Our Lady and had asked her to make them saints!

"That consecration is what Father Grignion calls 'The True Devotion to the Blessed Virgin Mary,'" observed Mary Louise, as she and her sister walked home from the poorhouse. "Oh, Elizabeth! Remember when you first told me of the sermon he preached about it at the Church of Saint Austrégésilde?"

Elizabeth smiled. "Remember? I should say I do! You weren't a bit interested. In fact, you were scandalized at the mere idea of talking to Our Lady as though she were a real person, or of thinking of her as your best friend. As for asking her to make you a saint. . . . "

"I know. I was terribly stupid."

"Oh, no! Not any more stupid than I was, because I had never thought about these things, either. But then—why should we have been concerned? No one had ever said a word about them before. In fact, I know I never heard one sermon that was just about the Blessed Virgin until Father Grignion came to town."

Mary Louise nodded thoughtfully. "Neither did I. Isn't it strange, when we do have so many zealous priests here?" Then, after a moment: "But there's something else that bothers me, Elizabeth. Three things, in fact. Can you guess what they are?"

Elizabeth shook her head. "No. What?"

"Well, first of all Father Grignion isn't doing a thing to help me to enter a convent. In fact, every time I mention the subject he just smiles and tells me not to worry. And then he tells me that the Blessed Virgin has a very important work for me to do. Imagine that!"

"*An important work?* But what kind of work?"

"I don't know. That's one of the things I'm worried about. Then finally—"

"Yes?"

"Last week I told Father Grignion that I wanted to make the Act of Consecration to Our Lady, the one that the women in the Wisdom Group have made. Well, he just wouldn't hear of it."

"*What?* But I thought he was so anxious to have everyone make the Act! Why, when I heard him preach. . . . "

"I know. But he says I'm not ready for it. He says I ought to pray and think about it much more, because it's so very important. In fact, to make the Act of Consecration to Our Lady is so important that it often produces some of the greatest graces a person can receive."

"Well, I suppose that's true. You shouldn't make the Act without first praying about it, and thinking what it means."

"But I have prayed and thought about it, Elizabeth! A great deal. And I'm sure I understand what it means. By it I give my whole self, body and soul, into the hands of the Blessed Virgin and ask her to make me pleasing to her Son—a real saint."

"Don't forget that you give her all the satisfactory merit of your prayers and good works, too."

"I know, I don't keep back anything."

"Even when you're dead, the satisfactory merit of the prayers and Masses people have offered for you isn't yours because you've already given it to the Blessed Virgin for her to give to others, if she sees fit."

"I know."

"And you're not afraid?"

"Afraid! Why should I be afraid?"

"Well, without any satisfactory merit, you might have to stay in Purgatory until the end of the world. Just think of that!"

"I have thought of it. But it doesn't bother me at all. When I come to die, the Blessed Virgin will surely look after me just because I have nothing of my own and need her help so much."

For a moment Elizabeth was silent. Then she turned impulsively to her younger sister. "I'd like to make the Act of Consecration, too," she confessed. "In fact, I think our whole family ought to make it."

Mary Louise returned her look eagerly. "You think they'd be interested?"

"Why not? We could talk to Mother about it. If we can convince *her*, the rest ought to be simple enough."

CHAPTER 7

PREPARING AND MORE PREPARING

WHEN the two girls talked to their mother, however, they found her not at all interested in making the Act of Consecration to Our Lady. In fact, she had very little use for Father Grignion, and lost no time in saying so.

"If you keep on going to confession to that priest at the poorhouse, you'll become as mad as he is," she told Mary Louise bluntly. "Why, the whole town is talking about his queer ways!"

"But he's a saint, Mother!" put in Elizabeth reproachfully. "You'd have to hear him preach just once to realize that."

"Maybe so. But why does he have to be so careless about his appearance? Patched clothes, old shoes, no hat—what's he doing with all the money from those begging trips of his?"

"Why, it goes to the people at the poorhouse, of course. Every cent of it."

"Well, there's no reason why he shouldn't keep something for himself. Why, he looks more like a common beggar than a priest! Really, the Bishop ought to do something about it."

Of course Mary Louise and Elizabeth were deeply disappointed at their mother's lack of understanding.

But presently they themselves were troubled when Father Grignion made an announcement that startled even them. Henceforth, he declared, he would not be known as Father Grignion. He would be Father Louis Mary De Montfort, or simply Father De Montfort, after his birthplace of Montfort-la-Cane. Never again would he use his rightful family name.

"I guess he's doing this in a spirit of holy poverty," Mary Louise loyally explained to her mother. "You see, he's never wanted to keep anything for himself, and so long ago he gave away all that he could—his money, the satisfactory merit from his prayers and good works, even that of the prayers and good works that will be offered for him when he's dead. And now—well, he's given up his own name."

"That's right, Mother," put in Elizabeth earnestly. "Father Grignion . . . I mean Father De Montfort . . . is really a holy man."

Madame Trichet turned away impatiently. "Maybe so, child. But he certainly doesn't appeal to me."

Tears crept into the eyes of Mary Louise. What a terrible disappointment that her mother did not understand! Why, Father De Montfort was the kindest person in the world! True, some of his actions did border on the unusual—such as giving up his rightful name in a spirit of holy poverty and going bareheaded in all kinds of weather. Then on occasion he had been known to speak quite bluntly to various people in Poitiers, especially when he had heard them using bad language or making fun of holy things. But even so, he had tried to make them see that he was not angry with them, only displeased and hurt by their actions. Personally he was their friend and always would be.

Realizing that there was little use in arguing with their mother, the two girls decided not to refer too frequently to Father De Montfort. After all, their mother was only one of many in the city who did not realize that

He had been known to speak quite bluntly.

he was a saint, and that he had arrived at this state
chiefly through his devotion to the Blessed Virgin.

"*She* taught him how to love her Son and to be pleasing
to Him," Mary Louise reflected from time to time, "especially after he made the Act of Consecration to her when
he was very young. Oh, if only he would let me make
it, too!"

But the weeks passed, and still Father De Montfort remained firm in his decision that Mary Louise was not yet
ready for the great grace of consecrating herself to Our
Lady. She must think and pray about it much more. Accordingly, Mary Louise set herself to a serious study of the
rather lengthy Act of Consecration which Father De Montfort had written, paying special attention to a certain passage in the middle:

> *In the presence of all the heavenly court I choose*
> *thee this day for my Mother and mistress. I deliver*
> *and consecrate to thee, as thy slave, my body and soul,*
> *my goods, both interior and exterior, and even the*
> *value of all my good actions, past, present and future,*
> *leaving to thee the entire and full right of disposing*
> *of me, and all that belongs to me, without exception,*
> *according to thy good pleasure, for the greater glory of*
> *God, in time and in eternity. . . .*

"That's the most important part of the Act," Mary
Louise decided. "When I have permission to say those
words officially, I won't belong to myself any more. I'll
belong to Our Lady. And she'll help me to be far holier
than I could ever hope to be by my own efforts."

But when would Father De Montfort give her permission to make the Act of Consecration—to be Our Lady's
slave, just as he was, and so win untold graces for herself
and others?

Mary Louise continued to pray and hope for the great

favor. Then, after a long period of silence concerning the subject, Father De Montfort suddenly announced that her time of trial was about over. She might make the Act of Consecration which he had written for those who wanted to be saints in the surest and quickest way possible. But first she ought to prepare for it in a fitting manner.

"*Prepare,* Father?"

"Yes. For twelve days I want you to say the *Veni Creator* and the *Ave Maris Stella.* Then read the Gospel of Saint Matthew, chapters five to seven."

Mary Louise nodded eagerly. "Yes, Father. And what else?"

"You might also read something each day from the Imitation of Christ. Perhaps chapters 13, 18 and 25 from Book I and chapters 10 and 40 from Book III would be the most suitable."

Mary Louise made a careful note of what she was to do. "Yes, Father. And after that?"

Father De Montfort smiled. "Don't worry about anything more. Just come and see me when the twelve days are up."

Mary Louise earnestly applied herself to the prayers and holy reading which her spiritual guide had suggested. But when the specified time had passed and she joyfully made ready to consecrate herself to Our Lady as her slave, the request was refused once more—gently but firmly.

"You've finished the first part of your preparation," Father De Montfort told her. "Now you may start the second."

Mary Louise could scarcely believe her ears. "But Father! Surely I don't have to wait any longer? Why, I've read the Act of Consecration dozens of times and I understand all about it! Really! And last night I even went over it again. . . . "

There was sympathy in Father De Montfort's eyes. "Yes, child, I know. But don't be misled. You've not gone beyond the surface of things. Why, even after you have made the Act of Consecration, you won't be grasping one-tenth of its meaning." Then, as Mary Louise stared in puzzled silence: "You see, to give yourself to Our Lady as her slave, to ask her to form Christ in you, is no ordinary devotion.

It's something so wonderful, so stupendous, that it's going to change your whole life."

For a long moment Mary Louise was silent, stifling her disappointment as best she could. Then she gave a deep sigh. "Well, of course you know best, Father," she said submissively. "What . . . what is it I should do now?"

Father De Montfort proceeded to explain. The twelve days just past, with their prayer and holy reading, had brought many graces to Mary Louise. They had weakened the spirit of the world within her, and had made her soul most pleasing to God. But now, by additional prayer and holy reading, she was to earn new graces for herself, especially during the next three weeks. After that. . . .

"*Three weeks,* Father?"

"Yes. Why, what's the matter?"

"But it's such a long time!"

"Not too long to prepare for one of the most important days in your life, child. Be sure of that."

Once again Mary Louise lapsed into silence. Then presently she ventured a final question. "What am I supposed to do during the three weeks, Father?" she asked earnestly.

Realizing well the struggle that was going on within his young friend's soul, Father De Montfort smiled encouragingly. "Here," he said, handing her a paper. "Take this home and read it carefully. It will answer all your questions."

CHAPTER 8

READY AT LAST

A T the first possible opportunity, Mary Louise read over the paper which Father De Montfort had given her. And to her great surprise she found that the prayer and holy reading required during the next three weeks were quite similar to what she had been doing, although with different ends in view.

Thus, during the first week, she was to aim at a better knowledge of herself, for contrition for her sins and a spirit of humility, rather than at the detachment from the world which had been the objective during the past twelve days. The prayers suggested were the Litany of the Holy Ghost, the *Ave Maris Stella* and the Litany of Loreto. The reading was to be chapters 24 and 25 from the Gospel of Saint Matthew, chapters 11, 13, 16, 17 and 18 from the Gospel of Saint Luke, and chapter 24 of Book I from the Imitation of Christ, chapter 5 of Book II and chapters 7, 8, 13, 20, 30 and 47 of Book III.

Elizabeth was frankly astonished when she discovered all that was being required of her young sister by Father De Montfort. "No wonder the poor man and his Act of Consecration to Our Lady are misunderstood," she said. "Why, most people would be frightened away by so much prayer and spiritual reading!"

Mary Louise agreed. "Yes. But do you know something?

I'm quite sure he doesn't require all this of everyone. For instance, those poor crippled women he's been helping. . . ."

"You mean the Wisdom Group at the poorhouse?"

"Yes. Some of them scarcely know how to read at all, and the superior is totally blind. Yet they've all made the Act of Consecration, Elizabeth. They told me so."

"Well, then, why is Father De Montfort making you go through so much?"

"I don't know. Unless it's some kind of test."

But as the days passed, Mary Louise realized that the prayer and reading assigned to her by her spiritual director were far more than a test. In some mysterious fashion they were bringing new light into her soul, so that she was conceiving holy thoughts and desires such as she had never experienced before.

"Now I know Father De Montfort was right," she told herself, greatly consoled. "I did need to pray and think much more before making the Act of Consecration to Our Lady."

With increasing eagerness she began the second week of preparation for the great event in her life. The prayers required were similar to those of the first week: the Litany of the Holy Ghost, the *Ave Maris Stella* and the Litany of Loreto, with the addition of the Rosary and a special prayer which Father De Montfort had composed in honor of the Blessed Virgin. The reading consisted of the first and second chapters from the Gospel of Saint Luke and the second chapter from the Gospel of Saint John. And both prayer and reading were to be offered for the intention of securing a better knowledge of the Blessed Virgin.

When the third week came around, Mary Louise applied herself with even greater zeal to the task at hand: the daily recitation of the Litany of the Holy Ghost, the *Ave Maris Stella,* the Litany of the Holy Name of Jesus and two special prayers which Father De Montfort had composed. The reading consisted of chapters 26 and 27 from the Gospel of

Saint Matthew, chapters 13 to 21 from the Gospel of Saint
John, and chapters 7, 11 and 12 of Book II from the Imitation of Christ, chapters 5, 6 and 56 from Book III and
chapters 1, 8 and 13 from Book IV—the special intention
this time being a better knowledge of Jesus Christ.

But just as the third week was drawing to a close, there
came a sudden and disturbing thought for Mary Louise.
"Maybe I still won't be allowed to make the Act of Consecration to Our Lady," she told herself. "After all, I still know
so little about her . . . and I do have so many distractions
when I pray and read. . ."

Such fears were groundless, however. "At last you've
begun to learn something about humility," Father De Montfort told her. "And that's all I wanted of you."

"You mean you'll let me make the Act, Father?"

"Yes. This very day. But first there's a question I'd like to
ask. And I want you to answer it as truthfully as you can."

Her heart filled with joy and relief, Mary Louise nodded
eagerly. "Yes, Father. Of course. What is it?"

"Tell me once again why you want to make the Act."

Mary Louise smiled. "So I can be a saint, Father. That's
all."

"But surely you can be a saint without consecrating yourself to the Blessed Virgin?"

"Oh, yes. But it will be much easier and quicker this way."

"Why?"

"Well. . . ."

"Tell me, child, and as simply as you can."

"Well, when I give myself to Our Lady so that she may
give me to her Son, when I try to do all my actions through
her, with her, in her and for her, I . . . well, in a way I *dis-
appear*, Father. I mean the bad part of me disappears, or
rather, it's very much weakened. I'm not nearly so apt to
commit sin as I was when I belonged to myself."

"So, once you've made the Act of Consecration you'll be

a saint and ready for heaven?"

"Oh, no! Just once isn't enough to make the Act. To profit from it really. I'll have to make it every day of my life—even several times a day."

"But won't that take a long time?"

"Oh, no. I'll use just the short form."

"The short form! What's that?"

"Only a few words, Father, *'I am all Thine and all I have is Thine, O most loving Jesus, through Mary, Thy holy Mother.'*"

"And what will you be when you say those words?"

"A slave. The slave of Jesus, in Mary."

"A slave! Doesn't that word frighten you? Or repel you in any way?"

Mary Louise shook her head vigorously. "Oh, no, Father! It used to do both, but not anymore."

"Why not?"

"Well . . . it's hard to explain, but since I've been praying and thinking about the Act of Consecration, it just doesn't."

For a moment Father De Montfort was thoughtful. Then finally he spoke. "You know, child, most people—your friends and family included—won't approve of what you're about to do."

Mary Louise agreed. "No, Father. But that's only because they don't understand. Why, to be the slave of Jesus in Mary is the most glorious thing in the world! How can I ever thank you for telling me about it?"

Suddenly a wave of happiness filled Father De Montfort's heart. What a wonderful day! Through the mercy of God another soul had finally discovered the precious secret which all hell seemed determined should remain unknown: that, generally speaking, holiness comes most surely and easily through complete union with and dependence upon Our Lady, the True Devotion to the Blessed Virgin Mary which he himself had practiced since his youth.

CHAPTER 9

MARY LOUISE'S VOCATION

THE next few days were happy ones for Mary Louise. How good not to belong to herself any more! To know that her own human weaknesses and failures were gradually being changed into strength and victories through the loving kindness of the Mother of God! Surely, as she had glimpsed long ago, to be the slave of Jesus in Mary was the most glorious thing in the world? It brought a real and lasting peace to the soul.

But before long came a great trial. In August 1702, shortly after Mary Louise had made the Act of Consecration, Father De Montfort announced that he must go to Paris. His young sister, Louise-Guyonne, who had been living in the capital for some time at the expense of a friend of the family, was about to become homeless and needed his help.

"The friend can't afford to support my sister any longer, Mary Louise. You must pray hard that I will be able to find a new home for her—especially in some convent, for I'm quite sure she has a vocation to the religious life. But since she has no dowry. . . ."

Mary Louise promised to pray, but her heart was heavy. Her spiritual director was going away! What would she ever do without his advice and encourage-

41

ment? And what about her own future?

"Don't worry," Father De Montfort told her, reading her thoughts. "I won't be gone long. And you will be a nun some day. Never fear."

But Mary Louise found this order hard to obey. Why did Father De Montfort always seem so unconcerned when she mentioned her own interest in the religious life? During the past year he had helped several young men and women in Poitiers to enter the seminary and the convent. Two of his own brothers were priests—Joseph, a Dominican friar; Gabriel, a secular. His sister Sylvia was a Benedictine nun at Fontevrault, and now he was going to try to find a place in religion for still another member of his family.

"But he never suggests that I go anywhere," thought Mary Louise disconsolately. "Oh, I just don't understand it!"

As the weeks passed, however, Mary Louise did her best to put away all anxiety about the future. Wasn't she now the slave of Jesus in Mary? And even if she hadn't made the Act of Consecration to Our Lady, wasn't everything that happened to her, or didn't happen, the Will of God? Of course! Then how foolish to worry, even for a moment, about what she was to do with her life.

"Still, it would be nice to know what God expects of me," she thought from time to time.

Then in January 1703, after an absence of five months, Father De Montfort returned from Paris. He had been successful in having Louise-Guyonne accepted by the Sisters of the Blessed Sacrament at Rambervilliers, in the province of Lorraine.

"Now, Father, what about me?" Mary Louise ventured to ask one day. "Do you suppose that these same Sisters. . . ."

Father De Montfort smiled, well knowing what was in his young friend's heart. "My dear, if you really want to

"Well, what's the matter, child?"

serve God in a community, come and live with the Wisdom
Group at the poorhouse," he suggested.

Mary Louise could scarcely believe her ears. The Wisdom Group? Why, these good souls weren't nuns! They
were only laywomen, and poor and sick and crippled at
that. Of course they were very holy, particularly the blind
superior. And they did an incredible amount of good at the
poorhouse. Still. . . .

"Well, what's the matter, child?" observed Father De
Montfort presently. "You don't seem very enthusiastic.
Don't you like the idea of living among God's poor?"

Something in these words made Mary Louise blush.
Surely Father De Montfort didn't think that she was too
proud to come to the poorhouse? That she was ashamed to
share the lot of his twenty crippled friends?

"Oh, Father, that's not it at all!" she burst out earnestly.
"It's just that . . . well, all this is so sudden! Why, I'd love
to come to the poorhouse and live with the Wisdom Group!
Really! The only thing is. . . ."

"Yes?"

"I'd have to ask my parents about it first. And I don't
think they'd ever agree."

"Well, go and ask them. Tell them that God's poor can
teach anyone a good deal."

That same night an anxious Mary Louise put the question before her parents. As she had feared, her mother
absolutely refused to consider the idea. Her father, however, who was a well-to-do lawyer, surprised her by taking
an entirely different view.

"I don't think it would do any harm for you to help Father De Montfort with his work," he observed mildly. "Last
week, just by chance, I heard him preach and he's a good
man, no matter what the gossips say about him. But just
what would be your duties at the poorhouse?"

Mary Louise shook her head. "I don't know, Father.

Maybe I'm to help the matron with the nursing. Then again, there's a lot of sewing and mending to be done. Perhaps I'm to look after that."

"And you really want to try this new life?"

"Yes, Father. I really do."

"Why?"

Mary Louise hesitated, "Well, because Father De Montfort is my spiritual director, and he suggested it. You see, for me he takes the place of Christ on earth. So when he tells me to do something, I know it's God's Will and I ought to obey."

Secretly pleased with his daughter, Julian Trichet remarked indifferently: "Well, then, go ahead and live with the Wisdom Group, child. After all, if things don't work out, you can always come home."

At this Madame Trichet burst into tears. "Julian, you must be mad!" she sobbed. "What are people going to say when they hear a daughter of ours is living at the poorhouse? Why, we'll never be able to live it down!"

Julian Trichet shrugged. "What does that matter?" he demanded. "If Mary Louise feels God wants her at the poorhouse, then no one is going to keep her from going. At least, not if I can help it."

Naturally Mary Louise lost no time in telling Father De Montfort that she had obtained her father's permission. But to her great dismay, she found him strangely unimpressed. In fact, once again he seemed to have lost all interest in the future.

"You'd have to have the Bishop's consent before you could come," he observed, frowning slightly. "And I'm not at all sure that he'd give it."

Mary Louise stared in astonishment. "*The Bishop*, Father?"

"Yes. Since you're not actually in need, you'd have to have his permission to live on the charity of the town."

Mary Louise winced. "But . . . but I was hoping to *work* for the poor, Father! Surely that ought to make a difference?"

Father De Montfort looked at her dubiously. "No, you'd still have to have the Bishop's permission. And since your father is a fairly wealthy man . . . and your coming here would mean an extra mouth to feed. . . . "

Mary Louise was hurt. It had been hard enough to explain things to her parents and to bear her mother's anger. It was even harder to find her spiritual guide, who had suggested all this in the first place, so strangely cold and uncooperative. But if she must also go to see the Bishop, a man whom she scarcely knew since he had been in Poitiers for less than a year. . . .

Then suddenly she glimpsed the truth. All these things were only trials! Father De Montfort was not being unkind or heartless. He really wanted her to come to the poorhouse. But of her own free will, and after having conquered certain obstacles.

"All right," she announced resolutely, swallowing her disappointment. "I'll go to see the Bishop, Father. I'll go this very day."

CHAPTER 10

MARY LOUISE'S NEW LIFE

THE Most Reverend Claude de la Poype de Vertrieu, the new Bishop of Poitiers, was astonished when Mary Louise came to him with her request. He lost no time in informing her that Father De Montfort's plan would never work. The daughter of such a prominent man as Julian Trichet would never be able to persevere as a member of the Wisdom Group. The meager food, the plain accommodations, the long hours of prayer and work, the lack of companionship with girls of her own class—all these things would be too much for her. As for coming to work at the poorhouse in an official capacity—well, at the present time there were no openings on the staff even for an experienced person.

Nervous and upset, and taken aback by the Bishop's brusqueness, Mary Louise did not try to argue her case, but timidly took her leave. In just a few days, however, she was back, filled with fresh courage.

"Your Lordship, couldn't you use your influence with the authorities at the poorhouse?" she persisted respectfully. "Even if there isn't an opening just now, surely there is something I could do for the poor? If you'd just write a letter and explain that the lack of comforts doesn't matter at all! That I really want to live with the Wisdom Group!

That I can always come home if the work is too hard. . . ."

The Bishop looked with renewed interest at his youthful visitor. Why, the girl hardly seemed the same person who had come to him so bashfully a few days before!

"Child, you don't realize what you're asking," he said kindly. "Why, you're only seventeen years old . . ."

"I'll be eighteen in May, Your Lordship—just four months time. And I've prayed and thought about things so much that now I'm quite sure what is God's Will for me. Oh, if you'd just write a letter . . . perhaps to the matron. . . ."

The Bishop hesitated. There was no doubt that he had made a mistake. Mary Louise Trichet was no weakling. She was firmly convinced that God was calling her to a life of sacrifice among the poor.

"Well, I suppose it would do no harm to ask the matron to find a place for you," he admitted finally. "After all, as you yourself have pointed out, it isn't as though this was something permanent. If things don't work out, you can always come home."

"Yes, Your Lordship," agreed Mary Louise happily. "Those were my father's own words."

Soon the Bishop's letter was finished, and Mary Louise eagerly set off for the poorhouse. This time Father De Montfort received her with evident pleasure, and took her at once to meet those in charge of the various departments. Of course everyone, the matron included, pointed out that there was no suitable opening for a girl such as Mary Louise, but Father De Montfort quickly set aside all such objections. Any work would do for his young friend, he said. She was enthusiastic and healthy, and she wanted no favors.

After some discussion it was decided that Mary Louise could be a junior assistant to the matron. However, she would eat, sleep and take her recreation with the Wisdom

Group. She would also give obedience to the blind superior of these twenty crippled women whom Father De Montfort had singled out to pray and suffer for souls. With them she would rise each morning at four o'clock, meditate for one hour, recite the five Joyful Mysteries of the Rosary, hear Holy Mass, then attend to whatever duties the matron assigned to her. At one o'clock she would recite the five Sorrowful Mysteries of the Rosary with her companions. Work for the matron would follow until half-past five. Then a half-hour's meditation with the Wisdom Group, concluding with the five Glorious Mysteries of the Rosary. Silence would be kept at all times, except during the hour of recreation after dinner and the half-hour after supper.

To the amazement of everyone, Mary Louise was happy in her new life. Of course there were difficulties. The working day was long, and certain tasks were not only tiring but repulsive. The food was uninteresting, and there were several among the poor who gave themselves to constant criticism and gossip, no matter what one tried to do for them. But Mary Louise was undismayed.

"I'm glad I came," she assured herself each morning as she knelt before the large wooden cross which Father De Montfort had erected in the living quarters of the Wisdom Group. "I'm only sorry it couldn't have been sooner."

Then late in January, when she had been living at the poorhouse for some three weeks, Father De Montfort made an announcement. Henceforth Mary Louise was not to wear the fashionable dresses which she had brought from home. Instead, she was to make herself a dress out of some plain grey homespun. And she would no longer use combs and ribbons in her hair, but would wear a white linen cap and black veil.

Mary Louise had misgivings at first. "I don't think Mother's going to like your idea, Father," she said respectfully. "She's always wanted me to wear nice clothes. And if she ever sees me in *homespun.* . . ."

"Why, what's the matter with good, honest wool?"

"Nothing, Father. Nothing at all. Only it is the material of the poor people's uniforms here, and . . . well, I'm afraid that Mother's apt to be offended if I dress like them and don't wear the things she chose for me when I left home." Then, after a moment: "Maybe, though, if I asked her permission first about wearing the homespun dress . . . *and* the cap and veil. . . . "

Father De Montfort smiled. "Well, go and ask her, child. It probably will save trouble."

CHAPTER 11

THE NEW DRESS

POOR Mary Louise! There was a far stormier session than she had expected when she reached home with her request.

"That Father De Montfort is mad!" cried her mother indignantly. "Isn't it enough that he has you living with the town's paupers? Must he have you dress like them, too?"

"But I won't look like the others, Mother," Mary Louise hastened to explain. "It's just a question of my having a grey dress, made very simply. . . ."

"Out of common homespun!"

"Well, yes. But it'll be the only one of its kind at the poorhouse. And far more suitable for my work than the clothes I took with me."

Madame Trichet dried her eyes. With all her heart she longed to refuse permission, and for an hour or more she had held her ground. But finally the fear of what her husband would say became too great.

"All right, go and make your homespun dress!" she burst out angrily. "You . . . you're no longer my daughter anyway. You don't seem to care how much you hurt me."

A pang shot through Mary Louise, and she was tempted to stay and console her mother, to try to explain things all over again. But what good would that do? Wouldn't it be

51

far better to return now to the poorhouse? After all, she had the permission for which she had come. . . .

"Mother, I have to go," she said hurriedly, her heart torn with grief at the lack of understanding from one she loved so much. "I've been away from my work too long already."

Madame Trichet's face was hard. "Well, go ahead," she said stiffly. "I'm not stopping you."

Mary Louise, discouraged and upset, hastened to report all that had happened to Father De Montfort. And he, when he saw how hurt she was, lost no time in consoling her.

"Don't worry," he said. "All this was to be expected." Then, with a little smile: "After all, child, don't you realize that the Devil is out to do all that he can to keep you from wearing your new dress?"

Mary Louise shook her head absently. "The Devil, Father? Why would he be interested in a piece of homespun?"

"Because of what it stands for, child." Then, touched by the girl's bewilderment, Father De Montfort went on to explain. The new dress which Mary Louise was about to make according to his directions was really a religious habit. At first she would be the only one to wear it. Later on it would be given to other young girls whom God would send.

"You will be called 'The Daughters of Wisdom,' child, and you will spend your lives in hospitals, orphanages, schools, bringing souls to a love of Christ by your works of charity. More than that. *You will help to make saints of those you meet by introducing them to the True Devotion to the Blessed Virgin Mary.*"

His words roused Mary Louise from the preoccupation with her mother. Could this be the work God wanted of her and to which Father De Montfort had made such frequent reference?

"I'm to be a *nun*, Father?" she demanded incredulously. "Here in the poorhouse?"

"Yes."

"Not . . . not all by myself!"

"Just at first. Then if it's God's Will that my plan should succeed, other girls will come."

"But . . . but I can hardly believe it!"

"Nevertheless it's true, child. Now do you understand why the Devil is so angry and is trying to put obstacles in the way? Why, this opposition from your mother is only the beginning!"

As though by magic, discouragement and sorrow vanished from the heart of Mary Louise. She was going to be a nun after all, just as Father De Montfort had always said! She was going to be the first member of a new religious congregation in the Church—the Daughters of Wisdom!

"Oh, Father!" she cried, her eyes shining. "How perfectly wonderful!" Then, after a moment: "When may I start working on my new dress?"

Father De Montfort smiled. "When? Why, right away. Come along and I'll tell you what I have in mind."

Soon Mary Louise was hard at work, and by February 2, 1703, her new dress was finished. Since this was one of Our Lady's feast days—that of the Purification—Father De Montfort announced that he would bless the new habit and Mary Louise might start to wear it right away. Then, although she was not yet a nun in the accepted sense, she might henceforth refer to herself as Sister Mary Louise of Jesus.

When the ceremony of blessing was over, Sister Mary Louise was about to take up her usual duties for the matron. "No," said Father De Montfort thoughtfully. "I'd rather you went for a walk through the town."

Sister Mary Louise stared at him. "A walk, Father? *Now?* All by myself?"

"Yes. You see, I'm anxious for everyone in Poitiers to

know about the first Daughter of Wisdom and to hear
what they have to say. And incidentally—"

"Yes, Father?"

"Be sure to walk up and down the main street. I want
everyone to see you."

Without question Sister Mary Louise made ready for
her walk, knowing full well what would happen. Within a
matter of minutes she would be the center of attraction for
scores of curious eyes. Men would stop their work, women
their shopping, children their play, to gaze upon her. There
might even be some who would laugh and make insulting
remarks, for in eighteenth-century France most religious
communities for women were cloistered and nuns were
seldom seen in public.

"What does it matter what people say or think?" she reflected. "This is what Father De Montfort wants—a kind of
Baptism for my new dress."

Then, walking resolutely through the front gates of the
poorhouse, she once again offered the prayer with which
that morning she had sanctified all she would do or suffer
during the day—the short form of the Act of Consecration
to Our Lady:

*"I am all Thine and all I have is Thine, O most loving
Jesus, through Mary, Thy holy Mother."*

"What does it matter what people think?"

CHAPTER 12

SHOCK WAVES FROM JANSENISM

SISTER Mary Louise soon found that she had not been wrong in supposing that her walk through the center of Poitiers, wearing the grey homespun habit and the white cap and black veil which Father De Montfort had designed, would create a stir. She had gone only a short distance when she began to hear the cries of the gaping townsfolk.

"Why, it's Mary Louise Trichet!" burst out one woman in astonishment. *"Julian Trichet's daughter!"*

"Oh, no! It can't be!" protested another. "She'd never be seen in an outfit like that!"

"That's right. She's always been one for nice things."

Her heart beating fast, her head held high, Sister Mary Louise walked swiftly on toward the center of town, ignoring the hooting of small boys, the barking of excited dogs, the stares of strangers, the amazed glances of friends and acquaintances. Up the main street she went and down again, while a jumble of voices echoed on all sides and necks craned from open windows and doors.

"Look! It's the Trichet girl from the poorhouse!"

"And she's wearing some kind of uniform, just like the poor people!"

"Why, she must be mad!"

"Maybe Father De Montfort's put a spell on her!"

"They do say he's mad himself."

"Quick, shut the door! Don't let her come in here!"

"Throw a stone at her!"

"No, no! Be careful! Her father's an important lawyer!"

"That's right. And she's not hurting anyone."

"But why is she dressed like that?"

"Maybe she *is* out of her mind. . . . "

Poor Sister Mary Louise! When she finally reached the poorhouse again, she was trembling and exhausted. In all her seventeen years she had never been through such a harrowing experience. But there was even more to come, for before an hour had passed Madame Trichet was at the front door, loudly demanding that she be allowed to see her daughter. Tears of rage were streaming down her face when Sister Mary Louise came to see what she wanted.

"You wretched girl! You're coming with me to the Bishop!" she stormed. "He'll make you take off those . . . those *rags*, and stay at home where you belong!"

Sister Mary Louise looked helplessly at Father De Montfort, who had accompanied her to the door. What should she do?

"Go along with your mother," he advised kindly, ignoring the baneful glances of Madame Trichet. "And don't worry, child. Everything's going to turn out well."

Father De Montfort was right. The Bishop, although he listened patiently to all that Madame Trichet had to say, declared that he saw no reason to order Sister Mary Louise to lay aside her habit and return home. In the first place, hadn't she asked her mother's permission to live at the poorhouse? Then, hadn't she also asked permission to wear her new dress? As for the fact that it was made of homespun, that the material had been purchased by Father De Montfort with an alms someone had given him—why, such objections were pure nonsense!

"Madame, you should be very grateful that God has

given your daughter a religious vocation," he said sternly.
"And remember this: she doesn't belong to you any more,
but to Him." Then, turning to Sister Mary Louise: "Go in
peace, child. And don't let anyone frighten you. You're
going to do a great deal of good at the poorhouse."

These words did much to console Sister Mary Louise.
Yet as the days passed and certain people at the poorhouse, the matron included, made slighting remarks
about her new habit, suggesting that Father De Montfort
was little less than a fool to dream of starting a religious
community with only one young girl for a member, her
heart sank. Repeatedly she told herself that she and her
spiritual guide were the slaves of Jesus in Mary, that they
had given themselves into the hands of the Blessed Virgin
in order to become saints, and that therefore she would
use the present trials to make them holy. Still, the
depressing fact remained. Father De Montfort now had
more enemies than ever before. Even many priests, good
and zealous in their own way, misunderstood and criticized him. As for certain influential people in town, until
now the most loyal and generous friends of the poorhouse—well, one by one they were falling away.

"Father, why is it?" she burst out desperately one day.
"Why are so many people trying to ruin your work?"

For a moment Father De Montfort was thoughtful. Then
he smiled cheerfully and shrugged his shoulders. "Sister,
did you ever hear of Cornelius Jansen?"

Sister Mary Louise shook her head. "No, Father. I never
did. Who is he?"

"The cause of all our troubles, I'm afraid. Because of him,
people are suspicious of everything I do, especially of my
sermons about the Blessed Virgin. And now that you've
joined me and there's talk of a new religious community
being formed—the Daughters of Wisdom—all his followers
are up in arms. They'll stop at nothing to spoil our plans."

Sister Mary Louise was aghast. "But Father! Why don't you go to see this man? Maybe if you talked to him and explained things. . . . "

Father De Montfort laughed. "I couldn't do that, child. You see, Cornelius Jansen has been dead for sixty-five years." And he proceeded to relate the unfortunate story of Cornelius Jansen, once Bishop of Ypres, in Flanders.

He had been a good enough man in his way, and a real scholar, but he had drifted into error. Before his death, in 1638, he had retracted all his errors, declaring that he wished to abide by the teachings of the Church. But unfortunately a book which he had written some time previously was published after his death. Of course it was condemned by the Pope and his Cardinals, and its circulation forbidden. Yet certain friends of the Bishop refused to obey this order, and gave the book wide publicity. As a result, much harm was done, for certain statements in the book gave rise to all manner of false teachings. Even now thousands of very good people were being deceived by them.

"One of those ideas is that religion shouldn't make us happy, Sister. Another is that we shouldn't pay much attention to the Blessed Virgin or the saints. In fact, the Jansenists—or the followers of Bishop Jansen—would have us believe that our holy Faith is something to be feared rather than loved. So, when I tell people that the Blessed Virgin is their best friend; that, generally speaking, the surest and quickest way to become a saint is to give ourselves to her Son, *through her*, as slaves—well, the Jansenists are horrified. That's making Our Lady too important, they say. Too familiar and lovable. She belongs in the background of our spiritual life."

Sister Mary Louise looked dismayed. "But Father, that's what I used to think!" she burst out after a moment. "Why, when my sister Elizabeth told me of what you said in one of your sermons. . . . "

"Yes, I know all about it."

"But . . . but I wasn't a *Jansenist,* Father! Why, I never heard of Bishop Jansen until now!"

"Not exactly," said Father De Montfort kindly. "And of course it wasn't your fault. Those who taught you when you were a child were to blame."

"But my parents are good Catholics, Father! They always saw to it that we children went to church regularly, even when we were very small."

"Yes, but what did you hear in church? Any sermons about loving Our Lady as a *real* mother? About thinking of the saints as *real* brothers and sisters?"

"N-no, Father. I guess we didn't."

"Of course not. And why? Because here in France the Jansenists are very strong."

Sister Mary Louise was puzzled. "You don't mean that there are *priests* who are Jansenists, Father? Here in Poitiers?"

"Unfortunately that's just what I do mean. There are dozens of them. And hundreds of lay people, too. But we mustn't think ill of them, Sister, no matter what harm they do us. Instead, we must pray for them, and ask the Blessed Virgin to enlighten their minds."

Then, as Sister Mary Louise was considering this thought, Father De Montfort announced that he was going away again. There had been so much criticism of his work by the Jansenists and many others that the welfare of the poor, even of Sister Mary Louise herself, was at stake. But if he went away for a while the storm might blow over. At any rate, he would be off for Paris within a few days.

Sister Mary Louise could scarcely restrain her tears. "But Father! What am I going to do all by myself?" she faltered.

Father De Montfort smiled encouragingly. "Exactly what you do when I am here, Sister. And don't worry. Everything's going to turn out all right. Just wait and see."

CHAPTER 13

SEARCHING FOR GOD'S WILL

DESPITE the encouragement which he had given Sister Mary Louise, however, Father De Montfort was worried. It was April 1703, and he had been working at the poorhouse in Poitiers for some seventeen months. Twice he had thought it well to leave, because of the troubles and misunderstandings caused by his enemies. And now for the third time he was taking what amounted to a forced vacation. True, he had accomplished some good. The poor were much better cared for now than when he had first come. Then Sister Mary Louise! Ah, what good she would be able to do some day with many consecrated souls to help her! But as for himself. . . .

"Lord, what do You want of *me?*" he prayed. "Isn't it to be a missionary? To go about France preaching to the people, and bringing many to know and love You and Your Mother?"

The missionary life! Yes, that had been Father De Mont-fort's secret ambition since his early days in the Seminary of Saint Sulpice. But after his Ordination in 1700 when he had applied for permission to go to Quebec, in New France, to work among the Indians, he had been firmly refused. He was not the right sort, his superiors had said. He would do more harm than good in Quebec, and end up by getting lost in the woods!

As he trudged along the one hundred and thirty miles to Paris, begging his food and sleeping where he could (since he had no money of his own), Father De Montfort smiled ruefully at his early dream. The New World certainly had need of missionary priests. But wasn't the same thing true of France? The mere fact that the Jansenists were so strong, that thousands of people could not read or write, that they knew little of the catechism because there was no one to instruct them, was proof of this.

"Dear Lord, I know I could do something to help," he reflected, "especially if I had a little company of poor priests to work with me."

But where was he to find such companions? After his Ordination he had preached a few missions and retreats in and around Nantes, but that experience had not been a happy one. The priests with whom he had worked had been so influenced by the writings of Cornelius Jansen that they had looked with alarm on any frequent or loving mention of the Blessed Virgin in a sermon. As for Father De Montfort's custom of distributing holy cards and medals at a mission, of organizing colorful processions wherein the people marched through the town holding lighted candles in their hands and singing hymns which he himself had written—this was entirely too much. It was making religion too familiar, they said, too childlike and recreational. In the end it would lead only to irreverence and abuse.

"Poor souls!" thought Father De Montfort regretfully. "Their ways and mine *are* different. It's just as well that I left Nantes when I did and went to work at the poorhouse. But perhaps in Paris I'll find some priests who think as I do. Then, with the Bishop's permission, we'll call ourselves 'The Company of Mary' and spend our time in giving missions and retreats. Yes, and we'll teach catechism to the children, too, especially in the country districts."

But when Father De Montfort arrived in Paris—shabby, tired and penniless—he soon realized that for the present the Company of Mary was to be no more than a cherished dream. For he had no influential friends in the city, and even certain priests whom he had known while a student at the Seminary of Saint Sulpice, good and zealous in their own way, gave his idea no encouragement.

"And chiefly because of the part I want *you* to play in it, dearest Mother," thought Father De Montfort sadly.

Yes, the professors of the Seminary were as suspicious of the plans of their former pupil, now a priest for three years, as they had been in the past. While all agreed that he was a holy young man, there was genuine regret that he was still so unusual in his ways.

"Mark my words, he'll do great harm if he keeps trying to get people to become the slaves of Jesus in Mary," insisted one. "That idea of consecrating oneself to the Blessed Virgin—well, it's just too different to be good."

"And unnecessary, too," put in another. "Why, I'm sure there must be thousands of canonized saints who never heard of it."

"Of course. The best thing for us to do is to leave Father De Montfort strictly alone. Probably he won't stay long in Paris anyway."

Poor Father De Montfort! It was very depressing to find himself still criticized and misunderstood by his former teachers. But he bore the trial as best he could and finally decided to apply for a position as chaplain and general helper at the Salpêtrière, the famous poorhouse in Paris where some five thousand needy men and women were lodged at public expense.

For a while all went smoothly. The authorities at the Salpêtrière were well pleased with the young priest who had come to them so unexpectedly, who thought nothing of working eighteen hours a day for his room and board. For one thing, he had a definite way with the sick and aged.

For another, sinners of all kinds were mysteriously drawn to him, so that within just a few days he had helped many hardened hearts to make their peace with God. Finally, his experience at the poorhouse in Poitiers had taught him how to manage a charitable institution most effectively and economically.

However, there were certain officials at the Salpêtrière who were jealous of Father De Montfort's success. Determined to get rid of him at all costs, they started a bitter campaign of lies and slander. When five months had passed, their efforts were rewarded. As Father De Montfort took his accustomed place at dinner one day, he found a curt note of dismissal under his plate.

Of course he was hurt. Yet there were no complaints. Evidently it was not the Will of God that he continue to work among the poor in Paris. Very well. But what was he to do then? And where was he to go? He had no real friends in the city. And seemingly there was no chance that he would meet a priest like himself, poor and eager to lead the missionary life, so that something might be done about starting the Company of Mary.

"Maybe God means me to pray and think about things for a while, rather than to work for others," he decided. So casting aside all worries, he cheerfully set out from the Salpêtrière to find some kind of quarters for himself.

The place to which Providence finally led him could scarcely be called a room. It was little better than a dark closet under a stairway in a dilapidated house near the Jesuit church. Its only furniture was a tin wash basin and a bed of two bare planks. In fact, it was so poor a place that it could not possibly be rented to anyone. It was used chiefly for storage.

"Don't worry. It's exactly what I've been looking for,"

In this poor cell he would pray and suffer.

Father De Montfort told the surprised landlord, who, believing that his shabby visitor was just another beggar, had offered him—in Christ's Name—the only free space in his house.

For several weeks Father De Montfort spent his nights in this strange cell, his days in the nearby Jesuit church. Every morning he appeared at a certain convent in the neighborhood where the Sisters, as ignorant as the Jesuits of his actual headquarters, gave him a meal. But the enforced idleness and poverty did not make him sad. Rather, they filled him with joy. For well he knew that there is always a reason for suffering. It is a priceless coin with which to purchase good things for oneself and for others. So, he reasoned, if he bore his present loneliness and hardship willingly, many graces would be coming his way. And sooner or later the Holy Spirit would make known to him what he should do, not only about Sister Mary Louise and the Daughters of Wisdom, but also about the Company of Mary, that little group of missionary priests which he hoped to found some day and place under Our Lady's protection.

But Father De Montfort's hidden life in his room under the stairs was not to be of long duration. By chance he encountered Bishop Bazan de Flamanville who had ordained him on June 5, 1700, at Perpignan. The Bishop, a kindly man, was in the city on business, but he was not too pressed for time to inquire what had happened to his young friend during the past three and one-half years.

"Father, begin at the beginning." he urged. "Tell me all about yourself and your work."

Father De Montfort was touched. How long it seemed since anyone had been interested—really interested—in what he was trying to accomplish! Soon, although he tried to keep back the more unpleasant details, he had told the Bishop his story.

"And now I'm here in Paris for a little rest," he concluded cheerfully.

The Bishop was not deceived, however. "My son, you've suffered a great deal," he said. "Things have been really hard." Then, after a moment: "I think I ought to take you to see Cardinal de Noailles."

Father De Montfort stared. Cardinal de Noailles, the famous Archbishop of Paris?

"But Your Lordship. . . . "

"There, there. Don't argue. I'm sure the Cardinal has some work for you to do. And important work at that. Come along. We'll go to see him right now."

CHAPTER 14

"FATHER, PLEASE COME BACK!"

TO Father De Montfort's amazement, Cardinal de
Noailles did have some work for him. And what a surprising task it was! He was to go and live with the hermits
of Mont Valérien (whose headquarters was on a lofty hill
overlooking the city) and help them to a better knowledge
and love of God.

"You know about these men?" inquired the Cardinal
anxiously.

Father De Montfort nodded. "Yes, Your Eminence. I
heard about them several years ago when I was a student
at the Seminary here in Paris. In fact, I've even visited
their church. But I'm not just sure what I could do about
. . . well, about helping them. After all, hermits are generally such holy men. . . ."

The Cardinal's face was grim. "You don't understand,
Father. Things aren't as they should be on Mont Valérien.
Months ago the hermits lost faith in their superior. Now
pride and jealousy have crept into the community. The
Rule isn't being kept, and unless something is done soon
to bring these men to their senses there's going to be serious trouble—perhaps even scandal."

Father De Montfort listened attentively to what the
Cardinal had to say. And though he was not at all sure

that he could help the hermits to achieve peace and good will, he promised to do what he could. Yes, he would go to Mont Valérien at once. He would live among the hermits for as long as was necessary.

To Father De Montfort's great relief, there was a warm welcome awaiting him when he reached the hermits' lofty dwelling place. Gratefully he realized that he was wanted, that the hermits were more than eager to have help with their difficulties. And when, noting his threadbare cassock, they suggested that he put on their white woolen habit to protect himself against the chill winds that blew about the hilltop, he was touched. Perhaps, through God's mercy, pride had not yet made too much headway in the community. Perhaps the work which the Cardinal had given him to do was not such a difficult one after all.

"If I can just win the hermits' confidence!" he thought hopefully. "Then surely half the battle will be won."

And what was the best way to win the hermits' confidence? Recalling his experience at the poorhouse in Poitiers, especially among the sick and aged, Father De Montfort decided that the wisest thing to do would be to listen patiently to every grievance which the hermits had against one another. He would put himself in the position of each one who came to him—agree that this or that brother was inconsiderate, harsh, ill-tempered; that life was difficult and certain parts of the Rule most repugnant to human nature. Never would he make light of the troubles brought to him, or seek to minimize them in any way. In fact, on occasion he might even praise his confidant for having persevered so wonderfully in God's service!

But when the complaints were all finished, he would bring out his time-tested remedy. He would point out, as gently as possible, that troubles exist everywhere, even among souls dedicated to the religious life. The best thing to do about them, the only thing, is to turn to the Blessed

Virgin for guidance. She, through God's all-wise plan, can make every suffering bearable, even understandable, if only one trusts her and asks her help. Not just once a day, or twice, but fifty times, a hundred times—in fact, as often as the soul is troubled and cast down.

"Yes, that's it," Father De Montfort decided. "The hermits must come to know Our Lady as never before. They must learn to think of her as their best friend, as being really interested in them, and able to help them as no other creature can. Then they'll know true peace."

Within just a few days Father De Montfort realized that his plan was bearing fruit. Slowly, surely, the hermits were beginning to find peace. There was no longer the same old bitterness between them. True, trouble did break out from time to time, but he was always able to clear it up in just a little while.

"I've won the hermits' confidence already!" he thought in amazement. "Rather, you have won it, dearest Mother! Oh, thank God!"

Presently, to prove to the hermits that their Rule was not so difficult after all, Father De Montfort began to follow it to the letter—fasting with his new friends, praying with them, working with them—pointing out from time to time, very gently, that pride had been the cause of all the recent trouble between them; that it is one of the Devil's chief tools for bringing souls to hell, but that it can be crushed, like any other vice, by the help of the Mother of God.

Then early in March 1704, Father De Montfort realized that his work was done. All was well with the community on Mont Valérien. Peace had been restored. The Rule was being kept perfectly, and he might now return to his quarters in the city to pray and think about his own future.

But even as he took up his former abode (the same poor cell under the stairs in the house near the Jesuit church), his thoughts kept returning to Mont Valérien. How good it had been to spend those weeks in the quiet countryside! To breathe the fresh air of the hermits' windswept hilltop! Then the Calvary on Mont Valérien—that huge outdoor group of figures and crosses representing the death of Christ between two thieves—how impressive it had been! How beautiful!

"There'd be far fewer sinners in France if every town could have a Calvary like that," he told himself. "If ever I'm allowed to be a missionary, I'll see that there are dozens of such Calvaries. The people will build them with their own hands at the close of a mission. And afterwards they'll go there frequently to pray—especially to the Mother whom Christ gave them when He died."

But when would he be allowed to be a missionary? And where would he find co-workers who were not Jansenists? Recently he had met a former schoolmate, Father Claude des Places, who would have made an excellent missionary. True, a year ago he had opened a school in Paris for poor boys who wanted to be priests—the Seminary of the Holy Ghost—and this project was now taking all his time. But it was not for this reason that he had declined Father De Montfort's invitation to join him in missionary work. His health was too poor, he had said. However, some day certain boys whom he was now training might be able to help. . . .

"That's all very good, but what am I going to do in the meantime?" Father De Montfort asked himself over and over again. "Dearest Mother, what *do* you want of me?"

Then, most unexpectedly, a letter arrived from Poitiers which seemed to answer everything. It was written by one of the men at the poorhouse in the name of his four hundred companions.

"Father, please come back to us!" was the constant theme. "Since you've been away, things have gone from bad to worse here. We need you—*desperately!*"

Father De Montfort read the touching appeal with mixed feelings. During the eleven months he had been absent Sister Mary Louise had carried on most successfully at the poorhouse. But now funds were running low. Many on the staff had found work elsewhere, and the substitutes were ignorant and unskilled. Even the Wisdom Group had disbanded because of death, illness and other reasons. Truly, things were in a bad way for all the poor in Poitiers.

For several days Father De Montfort prayed and thought about the matter. Well he knew that the poor loved him, that he would be able to make their lot considerably happier if he returned. Then there was Sister Mary Louise. Undoubtedly she needed him, too. But his enemies! What about them? Wouldn't they stir up the same old troubles all over again? Once things were reorganized at the poorhouse, wouldn't there be gossip, slander, misunderstanding, just as in the past?

Then suddenly Father De Montfort made his decision. The Jansenists would indeed do their best to ruin his work. They would make him suffer in a dozen different ways. But what of it? In God's all-wise plan, more suffering was probably the price that must be paid before the Daughters of Wisdom and the Company of Mary could begin their work.

"I'm going back!" he told himself, suddenly light-hearted and relieved beyond words. "I'm going back this very day!"

CHAPTER 15

SISTER MARY LOUISE'S DECISION

FATHER De Montfort set out for Poitiers without further ado. Shabby, penniless, but wholly at peace in his mind, he covered the one hundred and thirty miles on foot in less than a week's time. And what a welcome awaited him when he finally reached the poorhouse! Men as well as women wept openly. Bonfires were lighted in the courtyard. Even those on the staff who had been only too glad to see him leave eleven months ago came forward awkwardly to shake his hand. Sister Mary Louise wept in her joy and excitement.

"Father, you . . . you *did* come!" she burst out. "Oh, thank God!"

Father De Montfort smiled. "Did you think I wouldn't?"

"Oh, we did hope so, Father! But no one could be sure. In fact, the poor people didn't even know where to send a letter to you. Then someone suggested they write to Father Leschassier at the Seminary of Saint Sulpice. He would surely know where you were."

Father De Montfort nodded cheerfully. There was no need to tell Sister Mary Louise that for weeks his address had been a dark hole under a stairway in an old house in the slums of Paris. That Father Leschassier, his former director, now had little use for him, and that he had given the poor people's letter to another priest for delivery. That this priest, Father Blain, had searched for him for days without being able to find him. That when he had found him, he had been almost speechless at the sight of such miserable quarters.

"The letter reached me safely, Sister, and I came as soon as I could," he said casually. "But—should we talk any more just now? There must be so much to do. And people to see, too."

Sister Mary Louise stared at him. It was eleven months since she had had the chance to talk to Father De Montfort, and now—after just a few minutes—he was apparently ready to go his way without a single question as to her own problems! Why, she had not even begun to explain how the members of the Wisdom Group had drifted apart; how much trouble her mother was still making because she refused to give up her present way of life and return home; how certain people constantly made fun of her because she insisted on staying where she was when she could so easily join the Benedictines, the Dominicans, or some other time-tested community; how, because of such ridicule, no young girl wanted to join her at the poorhouse and so make possible the new Congregation of the Daughters of Wisdom. . . .

Then suddenly she remembered somewhat similar occasions in the past. Why, this was just another trial which her spiritual guide intended for her good! If she were wise, she would make full use of it.

"You're right, Father," she admitted honestly. "There *is* a lot to do. Some other time we'll have a talk."

Of course Father De Montfort was well pleased with the attitude of Sister Mary Louise, although he gave no outward sign. But he was far from being heartless, and in the days that followed she was always in his thoughts and prayers.

"The poor child needs a companion," he reflected. "Some one near her own age."

Then one day he made up his mind. He would go to see Catherine Brunet, an attractive orphan girl who lived in Poitiers with an older sister. Despite her fondness for dress, her love of dancing and popular songs, Catherine was really very devout. In fact, for a while she had lived with the Wisdom Group and had been of great assistance to the blind superior. But her piety was so well hidden that no one had ever guessed its genuine depth. Indeed, her lively ways had more than once shocked Sister Mary Louise. As for her habit of whistling, especially the more solemn hymn tunes. . . .

"I know Catherine has a religious vocation," Father De Montfort told himself. "And it's high time she did something about it. Why, by now she must be in her late twenties. If she waits much longer, God may take it away."

But when Father De Montfort called to see Catherine and urged her to join Sister Mary Louise at the poorhouse, she burst out laughing.

"You want to make a nun out of *me*, Father?" she exclaimed, her dark eyes sparkling. "What a joke!"

Father De Montfort smiled indulgently, "Well, why not? You've already had some experience in working for God's poor. And done much good for them, too. But just think what would result if you were to give your whole life to their service—*for His sake!*"

Catherine screwed up her pretty face in an expression of disdain. "Father, I'm surprised at you!" she exclaimed. "Don't you know I'm not the type to be a nun? Why, I'd die if I had to stay cooped up at the poorhouse all my life! And to have to look like Mary Louise Trichet, in a homespun dress . . . ."

"You don't like the habit of the Daughters of Wisdom?"

"*Like it?*" Catherine flung up her hands in mock dismay.

"The people here have no church of their own," he thought. "What's going to become of them when the mission is over and there is nothing to remind them of God and His Blessed Mother?"

At first there seemed to be no solution to the problem. Certainly the people of Montbernage could not afford to build even a small church, let alone to furnish and maintain it. Then presently Father De Montfort had an inspiration.

Suppose some building could be purchased for a modest sum and converted into a shrine to Our Lady? A place where the faithful could gather on Sundays and feast days for a few simple devotions of their own?

"Well, there's an abandoned barn in the center of town that might do, Father," suggested someone. "Of course it's not in the best of condition, but, if the owner would let you have the place for a reasonable amount, we could take up a collection and help to repair it."

Without delay Father De Montfort went to see the owner (who agreed to sell his property for a small amount), and soon everyone was hard at work. The men busied themselves with the carpentry and painting, the women with cleaning and decorating, and in a few weeks a really attractive chapel had been made out of the old barn. Then, quite unexpectedly, friends in Poitiers donated a statue of Our Lady—old, of course, and much in need of paint—but of definite appeal.

Father De Montfort was delighted when he looked at the newly arrived statue. It showed Our Lady as a queen upon a throne, the Divine Infant lying in her lap. And the face was so sympathetic, so kind and motherly. . . .

"Queen of All Hearts!" he exclaimed. "Welcome! Welcome to Montbernage!"

CHAPTER 17

THE YOUNG STRANGER

OF course the Bishop of Poitiers was delighted with Father De Montfort's work at Montbernage. This young priest had made not only the dozen converts for which he himself had hoped but had succeeded in having all the townsfolk receive the Sacraments, renew their Baptismal vows and then take part in dedicating a shrine to Our Lady! It seemed almost too good to be true.

"Father, now I want you to give a mission at Saint-Savin," he said. "Things are just about as bad there as they ever were in Montbernage."

Father De Montfort nodded understandingly. Saint-Savin was another poor suburb of Poitiers, without a church of its own, where the people were given over to vice of all kinds.

"I'll be glad to go, Your Lordship," he said. "With Our Lady's help, I'm sure I could do some good there."

So presently Father De Montfort was busy once again with the work he loved so much: preaching in the streets, teaching catechism to young and old; above all, bringing everyone to a better knowledge and love of the Blessed Virgin.

The result? Within a few weeks conditions in Saint-Savin had become vastly improved. Drinking, gambling

Once again he was busy with the work he loved.

and other disorders had given place to real virtue, and there was not a home where the Blessed Virgin was not loved and honored. In fact, the Rosary was now everyone's favorite prayer.

Naturally Father De Montfort was well pleased with the success of his second mission. What matter the cost to himself? That, in order to win God's blessing on his work, it had been necessary to do even more penance than usual?

"A missionary who doesn't suffer as well as pray for others is in danger of being a complete failure," he told himself resolutely. "After all, the Devil isn't going to stand idly by while souls are torn from his grip. He's going to fight doubly hard to get them back. And only suffering, *real* suffering, can win the grace of his defeat."

As he reflected upon his recent success, however, Father De Montfort's heart filled with fresh longing. If one poor priest could do so much for souls, what could he not do with one or more helpers? And yet the Company of Mary must still be only a dream, for even now he had met no priest with ideas actually akin to his! Again, despite his successful work at Montbernage and Saint-Savin, he knew that his enemies in Poitiers were watching his every move; that many of the clergy, being Jansenists, were stubbornly opposed to any mention of the Blessed Virgin in a sermon; to an emphasis on the Rosary devotion; to processions wherein the people sang hymns and carried lighted candles and colorful banners. In short, to all religious practices which appealed to the eye and ear and which he himself had found so useful in touching the hearts of the uninstructed.

Then one day as he was passing through the Chapel of the Penitents (which the Bishop had previously given to him as a headquarters), Father De Montfort stopped short. Kneeling before the Tabernacle was a poorly dressed youth, sunburned and travel-stained, a staff and bundle beside him. And he was saying the Rosary with touching devotion!

Much impressed, Father De Montfort drew closer to look at the young stranger. "He seems to be a country lad," he thought. "I wonder who he is, and where he comes from?" But minutes passed, and the youth continued to be lost in prayer. His eyes were shut. His cheap wooden beads slipped steadily through his fingers, and it was quite clear he had not the slightest notion that anyone was watching him.

Suddenly Father De Montfort made up his mind. This was no ordinary farm boy. "Son," he whispered, tapping the young man on the shoulder, "could I have a word with you?"

Startled, the young stranger looked up, then slowly rose to his feet. "Why . . . why, of course, Father." he said. And taking his staff and bundle, he obediently followed Father De Montfort from the chapel.

In just a few minutes he had told his story. He was Mathurin Rangeard, eighteen years old, from the nearby village of Bouillé-Saint-Paul. Recently a Capuchin Father had preached in his parish and ever since he had been thinking of becoming a lay Brother in the Order. In fact, this very day he was on his way to the friars' convent.

Father De Montfort smiled. "No, son. I think you're coming with me," he said.

Mathurin's eyes shot open with astonishment. "With you, Father? But I don't understand!"

"Of course you don't. Not yet. But you will. You see, Mathurin, I don't think God wants you to join the Capuchins, I think He wants you to join the Company of Mary. And only by coming with me can you do that." Then, as the boy's honest face continued to reflect puzzlement and disbelief, Father De Montfort began to explain that the missionary group which he hoped to found would need several Brothers as well as priests. And so eloquently did he speak

that soon young Mathurin was filled with enthusiasm.
"You mean that *I* could be your first lay Brother, Father?" he demanded incredulously.
"Yes. That's just what I mean."
"But . . . but you don't know anything about me!"
"No, except that you seem to love the Rosary. Tell me—do you say it often?"
"Oh, yes, Father. Every day."
"Why?"
Mathurin hesitated, overcome with a strange and sudden shyness. How could he explain, even to this kindly priest, how much he loved Our Lady?
"Well. . . ."
"Because of your family? Your friends?"
"Oh, no, Father! I don't know anyone who prays to Our Lady. Or who thinks about her, either."
For a moment Father De Montfort was thoughtful. Then he laid his hand on the boy's shoulder. "Son, wouldn't you like to bring many people to know and love the Mother of God?"
Mathurin looked deep into the friendly eyes searching his own, and suddenly all his doubts and shyness vanished. "Oh, yes, Father!" he whispered eagerly. "I would! But how could *I* do anything? You see, I've never had any education. . . . "
Father De Montfort smiled. "Don't worry about that," he said. "Just come with me and I'll tell you what you can do."

CHAPTER 18

A DISHONEST PLOT

THE days that followed were busy ones for Brother Mathurin. Not only did he accompany Father De Montfort on several new missions which the Bishop had suggested, dispensing rosaries, medals, candles, holy cards and other religious articles to those who crowded about his little stand before and after the sermons. He also prayed and reflected as never before, particularly about the Act of Consecration to Our Lady. For, like Sister Mary Louise, once Brother Mathurin had glimpsed just a little of its true meaning, he was on fire with eagerness to give himself completely to the Blessed Virgin so that she in turn might give him to her Son.

"Father, I like the word 'slave,'" he declared earnestly. "It . . . it means so much! When may I be the slave of Jesus as Our Lady was? When may I make the Act of Consecration?"

Father De Montfort smiled encouragingly. "Why, in a month or so, Brother. You see, it's best to pray and think a good deal before making the Act."

Brother Mathurin nodded gravely. "Yes, Father. I know. Because it's going to change my whole life. Even if I don't feel any different afterwards, there *will* be a difference." Then, after a moment: "How wonderful it's going to be! I'll give Our Lady everything, and she'll do the same for me.

Only she has so much more to give than I. . . ."

Father De Montfort was deeply touched by the innocent sincerity of his new helper. How many times in explaining the Act of Consecration—the True Devotion to the Blessed Virgin Mary—had he not found his listeners fearful, full of doubts, even stubbornly opposed to the idea of giving themselves as slaves to Jesus through Mary! Almost everyone he had ever met had had a certain unconscious pride in serving God in his or her own way. People believed in saving their souls and winning heaven, not with Mary's all-powerful help, but by dint of their own prayers and sacrifices.* The mere thought of slavery, even the Holy Slavery to Jesus through Mary, was something which thoroughly repelled them. Yet here was this unlettered farm boy, just eighteen years old. . . .

"Brother, I'm glad you understand so much so soon," he said gratefully. "But so that you may understand even more, suppose you say the *Magnificat* every day, slowly and carefully, and think upon it afterwards for several minutes? That will be a splendid preparation for making the Act of Consecration."

Of course Brother Mathurin was only too glad to do what he was told, and after some weeks came the great day when he was allowed to become the slave of Jesus in Mary. Kneeling before Father De Montfort in the Chapel of the Penitents, he recited the Act of Consecration to Our Lady with all the fervor at his command. And what joy filled his heart as he came to the principal part of the Act! Suddenly it seemed too good to be true that he, a poor boy from the country, could freely offer God, through His Immaculate Mother, a gift which no one else in the whole world could make—the gift of himself!

---

* Catholics know, of course, that their own efforts are not *just* their own efforts. A person's prayers and sacrifices are worthless for Heaven unless he has God's divine life (Sanctifying Grace) in his soul (see *John* 15:5). Thus, we can do good works to win Heaven only if God Himself is supplying the "heart" of these good works.—Editor, 1991.

*In the presence of all the heavenly court I choose
thee this day for my Mother and mistress. I deliver
and consecrate to thee, as thy slave, my body and soul,
my goods, both interior and exterior, and even the
value of all my good actions, past, present and future;
leaving to thee the entire and full right of disposing of
me, and all that belongs to me, without exception,
according to thy good pleasure, for the greater glory of
God, in time and in eternity. . . .*

Then presently there was fresh cause for rejoicing.
Because of the recent successful missions which Father
De Montfort had preached in the parishes of Saint
Radegunde, Saint Catherine and the Resurrection, the
Bishop announced that he might preach still another in
the Church of the Calvary. This church belonged to the
Benedictine nuns from the Abbey of Fontevrault (where
Father De Montfort's sister Sylvia had been a nun for
some five years), and was one of the largest in Poitiers. It
would hold at least two thousand people. And if more
should come, services could easily be held in the great
square outside.

Naturally the Jansenists were not at all pleased over
this decision of the Bishop. For weeks they had been watching Father De Montfort's missionary successes with growing concern, although so far they had made no real trouble
for him. After all, Montbernage and Saint-Savin were only
poor suburbs of the city; the parishes of Saint Radegunde,
Saint Catherine and the Resurrection not too important.
But now that there was to be a De Montfort mission at the
Church of the Calvary, in the very center of town. . . .

"Something's got to be done about this priest," they decided. "And right away. Otherwise he'll become too popular
with the people and make things impossible for us."

Father De Montfort sensed that his enemies were about

to stir up trouble, and confided his suspicion to Brother Mathurin. But the young man, in his inexperience, could not bring himself to believe that anyone could wish Father De Montfort ill. How could there be hatred of him, or a desire to interfere with his work? Why, he was a saint! You had only to listen to him preach to realize that. Or go to him in confession. Or watch him offer the Holy Sacrifice.

And what penances he took upon himself for the sins of others! Many days he lived only on bread and water, and the few hours of rest he allowed himself each night were always taken on the bare bround, with just a worn cloak for covering. . . .

"Everyone must know that Father De Montfort's the holiest man in Poitiers," Brother Mathurin hastened to reassure himself. "It's just his humility that makes him fearful there'll be trouble of some kind at the Calvary, and his words won't be blessed."

For the first few days everything did go well with the new mission. So many people attended his sermons that frequently Father De Montfort was forced to preach from the open doorway of the church so that the great crowd in the public square outside could hear him. Then when it came time for confessions, several priests had to be called upon for help. As for the outdoor processions, the public recitation of the Rosary, the singing of hymns to the Blessed Virgin—it seemed as though everyone in Poitiers was on hand for these.

Busy at his little stand with its display of holy cards, candles, rosaries and medals, Brother Mathurin smiled and nodded approvingly.

"Just as I thought," he told himself. "Everything is going wonderfully well."

But meanwhile the Jansenists were not idle. Having discovered that because of one of Father De Montfort's sermons some five hundred objectionable books and even

more objectionable pictures had been brought to him to be
burned in the public square, they were beside themselves
with anger. A giant bonfire in front of the church? Why,
this was scandalous! A disgrace! It was robbing the mission of any possible merit it might have had.

"That Father De Montfort is always trying to stir up the
crowd and call attention to himself!" they told one another
indignantly.

"That's right. You'd think he was having a carnival, instead of a mission."

"He ought to have more sense than to use such common
tricks."

However, the Jansenists well knew that they could not
actually stop the burning of the books and pictures. By now
too many contrite people were giving their support to this
extreme measure. But perhaps the whole affair could be made
such a mockery that the Bishop himself would intervene?

There was considerable argument as to what to do. Then
finally it was decided that a comic figure representing the
Devil should be made and secretly set on top of the books
and pictures to be burned. Then the Bishop would be informed of the ridiculous means which Father De Montfort
was using to stir up contrition and repentance at the mission. Naturally he would be very angry, and would come at
once to stop such undignified proceedings, whereupon the
people would be so impressed by the public rebuke given
Father De Montfort that they would lose all faith in him.
Then the mission would come to an inglorious end.

"But the Bishop's away," protested someone suddenly.
"The plan will never work."

"Yes, it will." was the answer. "Isn't the Vicar General in
charge during the Bishop's absence? When he hears
what's going on, he'll come to investigate. And that will be
even better, because he's disapproved of Father De Montfort's stupid ways ever since the beginning."

CHAPTER 19

THE VICAR GENERAL SAYS "NO!"

THE Jansenists lost no time in putting their evil plan into action. They made a vulgar, straw-filled figure representing the Devil, and on the day that the books and pictures were to be burned brought it to the public square.

"It looks more like a woman than the Devil," scoffed one man. "Why not give her some earrings?"

"Yes, and make them out of sausage," jeered another. "The fire will roast them to a turn."

The suggestion was received with uproarious laughter. Anything to make Father De Montfort appear more ridiculous! Accordingly, the stuffed figure soon had two sausages dangling from its ears, and amid hoots and jests it was lifted into place atop the mound of evil books and pictures.

"Now, who'll tell the Vicar General to come and see what Father De Montfort's been up to?" demanded the ringleader of the group.

"I will!" shouted a harsh-faced woman. "I've had a grudge against that upstart missionary for a long time."

But there was no need for anyone to hurry to the Bishop's house. Already a certain priest who tended toward Jansenism, horrified at the sight of the straw-filled figure and quite ignorant that it was none of Father

De Montfort's doing, was lodging a bitter complaint with
the Vicar General.

"Monsignor, there's something really scandalous going
on outside the Church of Calvary!" he burst out indignantly. "You'd better come at once."

In grim silence the Vicar General listened to what his
visitor had to say. Then he began to pace the floor. Father
De Montfort believed he was going to burn the Devil? Why,
he must have lost what little sense he had!

"It's true, Monsignor!" insisted the priest breathlessly. "I
myself saw the ugly figure. And I heard the people talking,
too. Oh, what a terrible day for the Church! And to think
that afterwards. . . ."

The Monsignor stiffened. Surely there weren't to be further indignities at the public square?

"Yes, Father." he urged impatiently. "Go on. What other
tricks has that . . . that *madman* up his sleeve?"

The priest glanced cautiously about the room. Then, in
a voice that was scarcely above a whisper: "He plans to set
up a huge wooden cross at the door of the church, Monsignor—a kind of memorial to the mission. Afterwards
there'll be a procession of hysterical women around the
square, with hymn singing and lighted candles and a lot of
new-fangled prayers to the Blessed Virgin. . . ."

Suddenly the Vicar General stopped his pacing up and
down. "That's enough," he declared grimly. "I'll soon put an
end to such antics." And summoning a servant, he ordered
his carriage to be brought at once.

By the time he had reached the public square, the Vicar
General's plans were in order. Scarcely glancing at the pile
of objectionable books and pictures, the stuffed figure of
the Devil, the giant mission cross a few yards away, he
leaped from his carriage and strode angrily toward the
church. The crowd gathered about the open doors paid
him little heed, for Father De Montfort was already

The ugly figure was brought to the public square.

preaching in the pulpit and every ear was strained to catch his words.

"Stop!" cried the Monsignor, elbowing his way through the entranced listeners and on up the center aisle of the church. "Stop that sermon!"

At once every head turned, and a gasp of astonishment ran through the congregation as the newcomer's identity became known. But the Monsignor was too angry to notice any commotion. A few feet from the pulpit, with a baleful glance at Father De Montfort, he suddenly wheeled about, his hand raised menacingly.

"By order of the Bishop, there'll be no demonstration here today such as was planned!" he shouted. "No burning of books! No burning of pictures! No procession! As for that wooden cross outside—someone take it away at once!"

As the Vicar General began to upbraid Father De Montfort for his lack of good sense, his stubborn disregard for dignity where religious services were concerned, his spiritual pride that was leading hundreds of people astray, the congregation sat spellbound. But Father De Montfort, once the first bitter shock was over, gave no sign that he was disturbed. On the contrary, he knelt meekly in the pulpit and with bowed head listened in silence to the unjust accusations. Nor did he lift his head until the Monsignor, eyes still flashing angrily and fists clenched, had stormed from the church and driven off in his carriage. Then, slowly, he came down from the pulpit—pale, but self-possessed.

"My friends," he said tenderly, gazing out at the sea of tense faces raised to his, "today we had thought to plant a cross at the door of this church. But it is not God's Will. Our superiors are against it. It will be better planted in our hearts than anywhere else. Let us plant it there."

Then, with a faint smile, he suggested that all join with him in offering five mysteries of the Rosary. And having given the crowd his blessing, he quietly took his leave.

CHAPTER 20

NEW HOPES

IF the Jansenists had hoped to destroy Father De Montfort's work, their hopes were vain. For the next day (which was the closing day of the mission) even greater crowds assembled. And when it was discovered that he had invited none other than the priest who had denounced him to the Vicar General to be deacon at the Solemn Mass of Thanksgiving, everyone was immeasurably impressed.

"It's true," one person told another. "Father De Montfort's a saint. We've never had a better mission than his before."

Upon his return to the city, the Bishop found himself siding with the people—especially when he learned that it was not Father De Montfort but his enemies who had placed the stuffed figure of the Devil on top of the objectionable books and pictures.

"Father, you've done good work," he said encouragingly. "Now I want you to give a mission at Saint-Saturnin. Things are in a bad state there. In fact, what goes on at the Garden of the Four Figures is a disgrace to the whole diocese."

Father De Montfort's heart filled with relief. In spite of everything, the Bishop was still on his side! Then the battle was far from being lost. With Our Lady's help he would give a really fruitful mission at Saint-Saturnin (another poor suburb of Poitiers where the people were slaves to vice of all kinds). As for the Garden of the Four Figures — that public park in the neighborhood where drinking, gambling and other disorders went on almost constantly—surely something could be done about it, too?

"I'll go to Saint-Saturnin at once, Your Lordship," he said gratefully. "And thank you—thank you for everything!"

Soon history was repeating itself. The crowds attending the misssion at Saint-Saturnin were even larger than those at Montbernage and Saint-Savin. Once again there was the moving spectacle of candlelight processions through the streets, the public recitation of the Rosary, the renewal of Baptismal vows by hundreds of contrite sinners. Even more. Shortly after the close of the mission, Father De Montfort succeeded in erecting a makeshift shelter near the Garden of the Four Figures which he placed in charge of some charitable women for the use of the sick poor. Never again would the public park be a place of sin and wickedness.

Of course the Jansenists were furious at such success. And when there began to be rumors that the most famous missionary in Poitiers possessed miraculous powers, that he had cured a number of invalids, including Madame d'Armagnac, the wife of the Governor of the city, they were beside themselves with rage.

"This priest is really dangerous!" they declared. "Why, he must be in league with the Devil to work so many wonders!" And they began such a campaign of lies and slander against him that finally even the Bishop grew uneasy. If Father De Montfort was really such a holy man, how could he have so many enemies? Perhaps there was some truth in these unfortunate rumors. . . .

"Maybe I'd better tell him to stop giving missions," he

mused regretfully. Then, as fresh slander reached his ears, he came to an even more painful decision. The young priest who was causing so much disturbance in the city had better stop preaching entirely! At least, in the diocese of Poitiers.

Father De Montfort was giving a retreat to the nuns of Saint Catherine's parish when the Bishop's tersely worded message reached him, and at first he could scarcely believe the dreadful news. It was now Lent of the year 1706, and he had been giving missions and retreats for only a few months. Surely it couldn't be possible that his work in Poitiers was finished! Surely if he went to see the Bishop and explained things. . . .

Then quickly he put the thought aside. The Bishop was a good and holy man, but most of his advisers tended toward Jansenism. The present situation was their fault, not his.

"The Bishop wants peace," he reflected sadly, "and there just isn't any peace when I'm around. Who can blame him for what he's decided to do?" And hiding his disappointment as best he could, he promptly closed the retreat to the nuns and returned to his house near the Chapel of the Penitents.

But Brother Mathurin was far from feeling such charity and resignation. By now he had come to realize that his beloved superior did have enemies, and strong and influential ones at that.

"Father, this should be stopped!" he burst out indignantly. "Every one of your missions has been a big success. Why doesn't the Bishop remember that and pay no attention to the lies and gossip about you?"

Father De Montfort smiled faintly. "Because it isn't God's Will, Brother." Then, after a moment: "Besides, it's part of the price to be paid."

Brother Mathurin stared. *"Price,* Father? What price?"

As simply as he could, Father De Montfort began to explain. That people should practice the True Devotion to the Blessed Virgin Mary by giving themselves, through her, to be the slaves of her Son—in other words, by making the Act of Consecration—was an extremely great grace. Of course Satan knew this, and therefore was determined that the True Devotion should remain as little known as possible.

"But God has a plan, Brother," continued Father De Montfort earnestly. "We—you and I—can help all manner of souls, even those yet unborn, to see the True Devotion in its proper light and make it their own, despite all the obstacles Satan puts in the way. Can you guess how?"

Brother Mathurin shifted awkwardly. "Do . . . do you mean by suffering, Father?"

"Yes. That's just what I mean. In God's all-wise plan, suffering has always been the best way in which to merit blessings for ourselves and for others. That's why He sends it to us so often. But the suffering must be cheerfully and willingly borne, Brother, otherwise it loses much of its power for good."

For a moment Brother Mathurin felt depressed. Then, slowly, his spirits began to rise. "You mean all this trouble we've been having lately—it *is* worthwhile?"

Father De Montfort laid his hand upon his young friend's shoulder. "Of course, Brother. Why, this very suffering can help to merit for friends and strangers alike the grace to practice the True Devotion to the Blessed Virgin Mary. To pay the price of that grace, so to speak. And that's all we care about, isn't it?"

Suddenly Brother Mathurin's eyes shone with new courage. "Oh, yes, Father!" he burst out eagerly. "That's all we care about!"

Then, even as the future began to take on more promise, Father De Montfort made a startling announcement.

In a few days he planned to leave for Rome to ask a great favor of His Holiness, Pope Clement the Eleventh.

"I want his permission to go to the foreign missions, Brother. I think that I—and you, too—could do more good for souls there than anywhere else."

Brother Mathurin could scarcely believe his ears. The foreign missions! "You mean we're to go to . . . to *China,* Father?" he exclaimed incredulously.

"Possibly. Or to India. Or to Japan. Or even to the New World. It makes little difference, so long as there are souls to be saved. Now, will you pray very hard that the Holy Father grants my request?"

Suddenly Brother Mathurin's heart was full to overflowing. What a brave man his superior was! How heedless of hardship or even of danger when it was a question of bringing others to know and love Our Lady and her Son!

"Of course I'll pray, Father," he said eagerly. "I'll say an extra Rosary every day for your intention—*and mine!"*

CHAPTER 21

WALKING TO ROME

ALTHOUGH the Bishop had now forbidden him to preach from any pulpit in the diocese, Father De Montfort felt that it would do no harm to say goodbye to his many friends by means of a circular letter. So, after a fervent prayer to the Holy Spirit for enlightenment, he set himself to penning a few lines to the people of Montbernage, Saint-Saturnin and other places where he had given missions.

With touching earnestness he begged all who had made these missions to be faithful to their good resolutions; to abstain from servile work on Sundays; to say the Rosary every day, receive the Sacraments at least once a month and do what they could to discourage bad language among friends and acquaintances. Then he urged that all join with him in prayer that the present pilgrimage to Rome might be blessed by God.

The letter finished, there was no need to wait any longer. Accompanied by a young Spanish student (who had earnestly begged leave to go with him), Father De Montfort set out on foot for Rome early in March of the year 1706. Allowing for visits at various shrines along the way, he would surely reach the Eternal City late in May. Then, God willing, he would have his audience with the Holy Father early in June.

"Dearest Mother, please bless this trip!" he prayed. "Let it bring many graces, not just for myself but for all those for whom I ought to pray."

Of course the young Spanish student realized his great good fortune in being allowed to be Father De Montfort's companion. What did it matter if the holy man insisted that they make the entire journey on foot, without funds of any sort, begging their bed and board as they went along? Providence would surely supply all their needs.

Yet after the first few days, the youth's courage began to falter. It was not so easy to lead a beggar's life; to suffer insults and misunderstanding; to keep walking when one was both tired and hungry; to sleep on the bare ground at night, or at best in some barn with the cattle. Naturally Father De Montfort realized all this, too, and did his best to encourage his young friend.

"My son, let's think of the good Saint Dominic," he suggested one day. "He was a Spaniard like yourself, and he made this trip to Rome many times—always penniless and on foot. And look what his sufferings accomplished! Why, he founded one of the greatest religious Orders in the Church! And he helped to stamp out the Albigensian heresy, too!"

The young student nodded gloomily. "Yes, Father. I know. But . . . but Dominic was a saint! He knew how to suffer well."

"And you don't?"

"Oh, no! I don't like suffering at all!"

Father De Montfort smiled. Not so long ago he had heard almost these same words from the lips of another young man—Brother Mathurin. Yet of late, through the practice of the True Devotion to the Blessed Virgin Mary. . . .

"Well, son, perhaps this pilgrimage will make a big change in you," he said consolingly. "Remember, there's an

old saying that no one ever visits Rome without becoming
much better or much worse for the experience. Much better, if he profits from the many privileges springing from
the presence of Christ's Vicar and the relics of countless
saints; much worse, if he rejects or makes little of them."

Then, as his young companion's spirits did not seem to
rise, Father De Montfort suggested that from now on they
ask Saint Dominic to guide and strengthen them.

"We'll offer his favorite prayer—the Holy Rosary—as
many times a day as we can," he said kindly. "That way,
he'll be sure to help us. And Our Lady will help, too. Why,
it could well happen. . . ."

"What could, Father?"

"It could well happen that we would be given the same
graces that Saint Dominic received on his pilgrimages. We
might even be helped to use them properly, too. And surely
that would be the greatest grace of all?"

As the days passed, Father De Montfort could not help
wondering at the sudden and surprising interest which he
himself had taken in Saint Dominic. In many ways (although their lives were separated in time by five hundred
years), his case and that of the Spanish friar were strangely similar. Thus, for years Dominic had yearned to found a
company of traveling preachers who would stamp out
heresy in France, but instead God had first led him to establish a community of nuns. True, there had been nine
women in the little convent at Prouille, as compared to his
one spiritual daughter in the poorhouse at Poitiers. And
when male helpers had finally come they had numbered
six—priests, clerics and laymen—in contrast to the soli-
tary Brother Mathurin. Nevertheless there *was* a simi-
larity.

Then presently an even more surprising thought struck
Father De Montfort. Saint Dominic's first trip to Rome
had not been undertaken in the interests of a new reli-

"But Dominic knew how to suffer well!"

gious Order at all! Rather, he had journeyed to the Eternal
City to ask the Holy Father's permission to preach to the
savage Tartar tribes in eastern Europe.

"Dominic wanted to be a foreign missionary, too, but the
Pope told him to return to France because he was needed
there to fight the heretics," he mused. "Could it be possible
that the same thing will happen to me? That I am meant
to fight the Jansenists in France? That I've been led to
think about Saint Dominic only to find inspiration in his
obedience when the time comes?"

But, as had been his custom from youth, he spent no
time in worrying about the future. Wasn't he the slave of
Jesus in Mary? Well, then, everything was in their hands.
They would take care of all that concerned him.

CHAPTER 22

AUDIENCE WITH THE POPE—
AND SURPRISES BACK HOME

AS he had planned, Father De Montfort arrived in
Rome late in May—tired, but gloriously happy. What
a wonderful trip it had been, particularly the two-week
stop at Loreto where he had had the privilege of offering
Mass each day in one of the most inspiring shrines in the
world—the Basilica of the Holy House of Nazareth! Then
the picturesque towns of Assisi, Perugia, Viterbo—what
happiness he had also found within their walls! But as he
knelt by the tomb of Saint Peter, he realized that the best
was still before him. For he was in Rome at last, with its
countless churches and shrines and relics of the martyrs.
And in a few days he would be face to face with Pope
Clement the Eleventh.

It was on June 6, through the good offices of the Pope's
confessor, that Father De Montfort found himself kneeling
at the feet of Christ's Vicar on earth. He had prepared a
little speech in Latin for the occasion, and had just begun
to read it, when the Pope laid a friendly hand upon his
shoulder.

"My son, why not speak in your own language?" he suggested kindly. "It would be . . . well, so much less formal."

Father De Montfort looked up with surprise and joy in

his eyes. What an understanding man the Pope was! How fatherly and sympathetic!

"Of course, Your Holiness," he said eagerly. And at once began to pour forth the story of his six years in the priesthood; his desire to instruct the ignorant by means of missions and retreats; his great love of the Blessed Virgin; an account of the True Devotion; his troubles with the Jansenists; the dream of helping others through the Daughters of Wisdom and the Company of Mary. Finally he expressed the thought that perhaps God meant him to do these things in some foreign land, rather than in France.

"It's for this reason that I've come to see you. Your Holiness," he explained hopefully. "Do you think I should go to the Orient? Or would it be better to go to the New World?"

Pope Clement looked at his visitor with keen interest. Then he leaned forward thoughtfully. "My son, how old are you?" he asked.

"Thirty-three, Your Holiness," Father De Montfort replied eagerly.

"You have good health?"

"Oh, yes! The very best."

"You really want to save souls, no matter what the cost?"

Father De Montfort felt his heartbeats quicken. At last the great moment had come! "It's what I've wanted all my life," he said simply.

With a little smile, the Pope lifted his hand in blessing. "Then return to France, Father. Preach, pray and suffer there. *That* is your vocation."

For an instant Father De Montfort experienced a shock of disappointment. Then the image of a Spanish friar, clad in black and white, flashed across his mind and he bowed his head in submission. So, he had been right after all! Like Dominic de Guzman, he was not to go to the foreign missions. . . .

The Pope had been observing his visitor closely. "Don't worry, Father," he said encouragingly. "Of course the Jansenists will make things hard for you, but all the same you'll do wonderful work." Then, after a moment: "You're to go back to France with more authority than when you came—as a Missionary Apostolic. Only take care never to flaunt the title. Work always in perfect submission to the Bishops of the dioceses into which you may be called. By this means God will give His blessing to your labors."

There was other advice which Pope Clement had to give, and Father De Montfort listened carefully. By now the first shock of disappointment had passed, and he was at peace. How good to know that His Holiness had no fault to find with his preaching methods! That he approved of the True Devotion to the Blessed Virgin Mary! That he had given authority to impart the Papal Benediction at the close of every mission and retreat! That he had blessed a small ivory crucifix brought from France so that now all who kissed it at the hour of death, while being truly contrite for their sins and invoking the Names of Jesus and Mary, might receive a plenary indulgence. . . .

Without delay he set about the return trip, the ivory crucifix fastened securely into the top of his traveler's staff. What work lay ahead he did not know. Possibly the Bishop of Poitiers had had a change of heart during his absence and now would permit him to take up missionary work again. Yet what about the Bishop's friends and advisers? Surely it was too much to hope that they would be in favor of his return. . . .

"Still, it won't do any harm to see what's been happening in Poitiers," Father De Montfort decided. "After all, I did promise Brother Mathurin to meet him there."

So, despite the summer heat, the new Missionary Apostolic doggedly made his way back to Poitiers, and on the morning of August 25, the feast of his patron, Saint Louis of France, he arrived at Ligugé, a suburb some five miles outside the city. Anxious to offer Mass, and knowing that the Jesuit Fathers would be glad to see him, he went at once to their church. And here, to his great surprise, he met Brother Mathurin. Yet when the greetings were over and he had offered the Holy Sacrifice, he sensed a certain uneasiness in his young follower. And among the Jesuit Fathers, too. Conversation did not flow easily. All seemed to be looking at him as though they had never seen him before.

"Well, what's the trouble?" he asked cheerfully. "Brother Mathurin, your eyes are as big as saucers. Is something wrong?"

The young man hesitated. How could he put into words all that was in his heart? Why, his beloved superior had aged at least ten years since his departure for Rome! Burned by the sun and wind, he was even shabbier than usual. And so dreadfully thin! Then, too, he had developed a painful limp from so much walking. . . .

"N-nothing's wrong, Father," he stammered. "It's just that you look so . . . so different. *And* tired."

Father De Montfort laughed. "Different? Tired? Brother, I never felt better in my life. Come, it's time we got started for the city. I want to see the Bishop as soon as I can."

At these words, the Jesuit Fathers looked at one another uneasily. Then the Superior quickly suggested that the visit be postponed for a while.

"You've come a long way, Father," he said. "Why not have a good rest before going into the city?"

Father De Montfort was not deceived. So—there *was* some kind of trouble! His enemies had been busy during his absence and had poisoned the Bishop's mind against him still further.

"No, I think I ought to see His Lordship right away," he said. "Come, Brother." And having thanked the Jesuits for their hospitality, he set out for Poitiers without asking any questions. But in just a little while he had turned curiously to his young companion.

"Brother, tell me everything," he urged. "What's been happening here these last five months? Why were you waiting for me at Ligugé, instead of at the Chapel of the Penitents in the city?"

Brother Mathurin swallowed hard. What was the use of trying to evade the issue? To explain that the trip to see the Bishop was useless?

"Father, His Lordship doesn't want you around any more!" he blurted out. "He's taken back the Chapel of the Penitents. And the house, too. I . . . I don't think he'll even let you say Mass in the city. Look, couldn't we go back to Ligugé? It's five miles to the Bishop's house, and you're limping so badly. . . ."

Father De Montfort stopped. The Bishop had forbidden him to offer Mass in Poitiers? Surely his enemies hadn't gone that far with their lies and slander!

Or had they?

CHAPTER 23

HELPING TO MAKE SAINTS

DESPITE Brother Mathurin's fervent pleading, Father De Montfort decided to continue on to the city. And here his worst fears were realized. The Bishop informed him, coldly, that there was no longer a place for him in Poitiers. Not only was he forbidden to offer Mass in any church or chapel. He must leave the city within twenty-four hours.

"You've done more harm than good, Father," he said. "There's been nothing but trouble and unpleasantness ever since you came."

Poor Father De Montfort! The Bishop's words cut him to the quick. Yet he made no excuses for himself. Nor did he protest that Pope Clement the Eleventh approved of his preaching methods, and had just sent him back to France as a Missionary Apostolic. No, the Bishop was a good and holy man, and he was doing only what he believed to be right. If anyone was to blame for the present misunderstanding, it was the Jansenists who were the Bishop's friends and advisers.

But what to do now? And where to go? In the end, Father De Montfort decided to visit a priest-friend who lived some eighteen miles outside the city. He would ask him for a week's hospitality, during which time he would pray for light concerning the future.

Brother Mathurin protested. Set out on foot on an eighteen-mile trip when it was almost noon and the August heat at its worst? Why, this was enough to kill any man, let alone one who was lame and worn after a difficult pilgrimage to Rome! Surely it would be far better to spend the day in Poitiers with the Jesuit Fathers (still their loyal friends), then make plans for the future?

Father De Montfort smiled faintly. "And run the risk of not having a place to say Mass in the morning? Oh no, Brother. That will never do. Come along."

Then, as he had done so many times in the past, Father De Montfort set himself to raising the spirits of his young follower. This present suffering was not without point, he said. Providence had sent it to them so that they might merit many graces for themselves and others. For instance, because of their hardships on this eighteen-mile walk in the hot sun, over rough country roads, surely someone, somewhere, was receiving the grace to overcome a temptation? Then the True Devotion to the Blessed Virgin Mary! Undoubtedly it also was being practiced through the merits of this present trial.

"Remember what I told you not so long ago, Brother? To make the Act of Consecration to Our Lady and so become the slave of Jesus in Mary is one of the greatest graces that a person can receive. But the price is very high. And seemingly God has let us be among the first to pay it—for ourselves and others."

Brother Mathurin nodded gloomily. "Yes, Father. I know. But if only we could be sure. . . ."

"Sure of what, Brother?"

"Well, that people appreciate what we're doing for them. For instance, if we just knew how many there are! And who they are! Or what might happen to them if we *didn't* suffer, and if they *didn't* know about the Act of

Consecration to Our Lady. . . . "

Father De Montfort smiled understandingly. "You think that would help?"

"Oh, yes, Father! I know it would!"

Suddenly Father De Montfort stopped and pointed to a wide valley shimmering before them in the noonday sun, His face was radiant. "Brother, some day, if you and I do what God asks of us, we'll go to heaven. And with us and after us will come more men, women and children than that valley can hold. And they'll be there chiefly because of the graces that came their way when they learned about the Act of Consecration to Our Lady from us—*and made it!*"

Brother Mathurin stared. "You mean all these people will go to heaven just because of what we have to tell them about the True Devotion to the Blessed Virgin Mary?"

"Yes. Only let's put it this way. They'll go there *more easily* because of that, Brother."

"And if we don't tell them?"

"Then certainly some will have to spend a very long time in Purgatory. And others—although it's a hard thing to say—may never reach heaven at all."

Brother Mathurin could scarcely believe his ears. Why, the valley could hold thousands of people! Even hundreds of thousands! And if the salvation of all these souls depended, even in a small measure, on the part he had to play in telling others of Our Lady's way of making saints. . . .

"Father, if we could just know who some of these people are!" he persisted. "Where they live . . . what they're doing now. . . ."

A soft light crept into Father De Montfort's eyes as he, too, looked out upon the valley. "My son, huge numbers of those people you're thinking about aren't even born," he declared earnestly. "They belong to future times—to the

Why, the valley could hold thousands of people!

nineteenth century, even to the twentieth. . . ."

Brother Mathurin's eyes shot open with astonishment. *"The twentieth century,* Father? Oh, no!"

"And why not?"

"But that's too far away! Why, we'll both be dead and buried even before this eighteenth century is over!"

"No matter. Through God's mercy, you and I can pay the price for future generations to know and love the True Devotion to the Blessed Virgin Mary. And as for all these people being grateful to us for helping them to get to heaven more easily—well, can you imagine a saint, a perfect soul—not knowing how to say 'thank you'?"

Suddenly new courage filled Brother Mathurin's heart. Father De Montfort spoke so convincingly!

"You're right, Father," he admitted. "There *is* a good reason for all these troubles of ours, just as you say."

Presently the future took on fresh promise. Following an eight-day retreat at the house of his priest-friend outside Poitiers, Father De Montfort announced that they would be going to Brittany. After pilgrimages to the famous shrine of Our Lady at Saumur and that of Saint Michael off the west coast of France, they would seek an audience with some Bishop and ask for missionary work.

Brother Mathurin's eyes shone, Brittany! Why, this western province was the birthplace of Father De Montfort! Here lived his parents, his brothers and sisters and those who had known him since childhood. Surely a royal welcome would await the two of them at Rennes, Dinan and other Breton towns? Surely, at least for a little while, there would be no more trials and troubles?

CHAPTER 24

DISCOVERED!

THE travelers did receive a warm welcome in Brittany, and on the way there, too, particularly in Saumur at the convent of the Sisters of Saint Anne of Providence. Then at Rennes there was a happy meeting with Father De Montfort's aged parents and a priest-uncle. For two busy weeks, at the invitation of the local authorities, there was a constant round of preaching in various churches, as well as in the two seminaries of the town. Greatly encouraged, Brother Mathurin would have been quite content to remain in Rennes, but Father De Montfort did not feel that this was God's Will.

"We ought to go to Dinan as soon as possible, Brother," he announced one day. "I'm sure we owe that much to Blessed Alan."

Once Brother Mathurin would have been quite puzzled at such a statement, but not now. For Blessed Alan de la Roche, who had died in 1475, was one of Father De Montfort's favorite heavenly friends. What was more natural than that he should want to visit the famous shrine at Dinan dedicated to this zealous Dominican friar who had spent much of his lifetime of forty-seven years in promoting devotion to Our Lady by means of the Holy Rosary?

It was on the Feast of All Saints of that same year, 1706, that master and disciple started the thirty-mile journey to Dinan. Brother Mathurin was more than ordinarily excited, for he felt sure that they would spend the night at Montfort-la-Cane, Father De Montfort's birthplace. Once again, as at Rennes, there would be the chance to meet those who had known his beloved superior since childhood, and who could tell many interesting stories about him. But presently he found that Father De Montfort had other plans. They would not interrupt their journey by stopping at Montfort-la-Cane. Instead, they would spend the night at La Bacheleraie, an obscure village about a mile and one-half distant. And they would do so as complete strangers—without telling anyone who they were—at least, not right away.

Naturally Brother Mathurin was disappointed, but his spirits rose when he learned that Father De Montfort's childhood nurse, an old woman named Andrée, lived in La Bacheleraie, and that they would ask hospitality from her.

"At least she'll be able to tell me something about the past," he reflected.

Darkness was falling when the two travelers arrived at Andrée's house. Still under strict orders not to reveal his identity, or that of his companion waiting in the shadows, Brother Mathurin stepped up to the threshold. He was to act as though they were two poor beggars who needed food and lodging for the night. The good Andrée would ask no questions, and thus merit far more for her kindness than if she had known who her visitors really were. Later, of course, Father De Montfort would reveal his little joke. Then, what rejoicing! What happiness for all!

But to Brother Mathurin's great dismay, it was not Andrée who answered his knock but her son-in-law—a grim-faced man with an uncertain temper.

"Bed and board for two tramps?" he snapped indignantly, as Brother Mathurin made known his needs. "I should say not! Be off with you, fool!" And with a muttered oath, he slammed the door and made it fast.

Brother Mathurin could scarcely believe his ears, and was on the point of knocking again when Father De Montfort shook his head. "No, Brother, we'll try another house," he said gently. "Can't you see we're not wanted here?"

However, within a few minutes it was evident that no one else in La Bacheleraie would shelter two homeless men either. Apparently there was nothing to do but spend the chill November night in the open. Then suddenly Father De Montfort had an idea. Inquiry had already revealed that the poorest person in the village was an old man named Peter Belin. Perhaps if they asked him for a little food and a place to sleep. . . .

Of course old Peter was surprised when the two travelers presented themselves with their request. But he did not turn them away.

"Sirs, I have only the floor to offer you for a bed," he confessed. "And not much more than bread and water for your supper. But you're very welcome to what I have."

Brother Mathurin looked hopefully at Father De Montfort. By the light of Peter's candle he could see that the old man's shack was in poor repair, but that it was also neat and clean. And there was something about Peter himself, a certain kindness and grace. . . .

Father De Montfort smilingly returned his companion's hopeful glance. Then he laid his hand on the old man's shoulder. How well he remembered Peter! How often he had spoken with him as a child! But of course the old man did not recognize him, for twenty-one years had passed since Louis Mary Grignion, a boy of twelve, had left these parts to enter the Jesuit College in Rennes. And now on this chill November night, wrapped in an ample traveling cloak that completely hid his priestly attire. . . .

"My friend, we'll be more than happy to stay with you,"
he said. "May the Lord reward you for your kindness."

In just a few minutes, after a painfully frugal supper,
Brother Mathurin had stretched himself out on the clean
straw which Peter had spread on the floor. How tired he
was! And how good not to have to spend the night in the
open! But in what seemed an incredibly short time he was
awakened by bright sunlight streaming in his eyes and a
babble of eager voices in his ears.

With a start he sat up. Father De Montfort was nowhere
to be seen, but the door of Peter's shack was open wide and
a dozen or more excited people were milling about in the
yard!

"God be praised! Louis Mary Grignion's come back!"

"*Father* Grignion, you mean."

"Yes, and he spent the whole night in this wretched
place!"

"Oh, what a shame!"

"Well, from now on he'll fare better. He'll stay with us."

"No, no! He's coming to our house!"

"Maybe so. But first he ought to eat something."

"Yes. Look, Father—here's some bread and cheese. . . . "

"And some good wine to go with it. . . . "

"What about a warmer cloak, Father?"

"And one for your friend, too?"

Puzzled, Brother Mathurin scrambled to his feet and
hurried to the door. What could have happened? What was
going on in Peter's front yard? Then he stopped short in
amazement. A few feet away was Father De Montfort—
smiling and quite at ease—surrounded by the very ones
who a few hours before could not be bothered with him!
And an old woman, crying and laughing at the same time,
was clinging to his arm as though she would never let him
go.

"Andrée!" thought Brother Mathurin. "Father's old

nurse!" Then, after a moment: "But how did she or anyone else know that we were here?"

Soon part of the story was out. Late the night before, the memory which had been nagging at Peter Belin's mind became clear to him and he stumbled onto the truth. The elder of his visitors was surely a Grignion. In fact, he was none other than Louis Mary, son of John Baptist Grignion, owner of much property in La Bacheleraie! Father De Montfort had acknowledged this, and of course nothing would do but that Peter have his priestly blessing at once, and permission to spread the good news of his return at the first light of dawn.

Brother Mathurin made what he could out of this and various other snatches of conversation. Then presently . . .

"Father, you must come and stay with us!" insisted Andrée tearfully. "Oh, if I'd just been home when you came to the door last night! But I was away visiting a neighbor. . . . "

Father De Montfort nodded cheerfully. "It's all right, Andrée, Don't worry about last night."

"Then you do forgive us? You will come and stay at the house?"

"I'm afraid not. Brother Mathurin and I are leaving this morning for Dinan."

Suddenly Andrée began to sob as though her heart would break. "But surely you could come for a little while, Father! For a meal, at least. . . ."

After a moment's hesitation, Father De Montfort put an arm about his old nurse. "All right, Andrée. Brother Mathurin and I will come for dinner. After that we'll leave for Dinan."

CHAPTER 25

THE GRUMPY BROTHER

THE visit with Andrée passed much too quickly for Brother Mathurin's liking. How many stories the old woman had to tell of Father De Montfort's younger days! For instance, there was the touching one of the friendship of the boy Louis with his young sister Guyonne-Louise—now Sister Mary Catherine of Saint Bernard at the convent of the Sisters of the Blessed Sacrament in Rambervilliers.

"Look, my little sister, you will always be pretty, and everyone will love you, if you will only do your best to love God," he had told her over and over again. And when, on occasion, the little girl had balked at saying her prayers, he had coaxed her into doing so with small gifts.

Then, when young Louis was at school with the Jesuits in Rennes, he had shown a remarkable skill for drawing and painting. He had even sold one of his works—a painting of the Child Jesus with Saint John the Baptist—to an important lawyer. Again, while still at school in Rennes, he had been so touched by the plight of a fellow-student who had no decent clothes that he had secretly taken up a collection for him. This did not yield enough money to buy his friend a suit, but young Louis had prevailed upon a charitable tailor to provide one. Then some years later, while studying at a private seminary in Paris, he had helped pay for his tuition by taking on a duty which appealed to very few young men—that of keeping watch by the side of the dead several nights a week. Four hours of this time were given to prayer; two hours to spiritual reading; two to sleep and the time that remained to study. "I could have learned a lot more about Father De Montfort's younger days if we'd just stayed a bit longer in La Bacheleraie," reflected Brother Mathurin, as they resumed their journey to Dinan. "But no—it seems that Blessed Alan expects us at his shrine."

Blessed Alan de la Roche! As they walked along the remaining sixteen miles to Dinan, Father De Montfort talked enthusiastically about the holy Dominican friar. What a wonderful preacher he had been! How he had loved the Blessed Virgin! Why, several times she had actually appeared to him and made a number of promises concerning the rewards in store for those who said the Rosary devoutly! Thus:

To all who recite my Rosary devoutly, I promise my special protection and very great graces.

Those who recite my Rosary piously, considering its mysteries, will not be overwhelmed by misfortune or die a bad death.

I will deliver very promptly from Purgatory the souls devoted to my Rosary.

What you shall ask through the Rosary, you shall obtain.

"I hope to offer several Masses at the shrine of Blessed Alan in the Dominican church," said Father De Montfort presently. "And to have a visit with my brother Joseph, too. He's a Dominican friar, you know, and stationed in Dinan."

Brother Mathurin nodded eagerly. Andrée had already confided that Father Joseph Peter Grignion was an eminent member of the Order of Friars Preachers. How happy he would be to see his older brother once again! But on reaching Dinan, a great disappointment awaited Brother Mathurin. For it was not to the Dominicans that Father De Montfort applied for hospitality but to a poor community of priests—the Fathers of the Mission. And only after several days did he seem to remember his great desire of praying at the shrine of Blessed Alan and visiting Father Joseph Peter. Then one morning—

"I'm going to offer Mass at the Dominican church today," he announced. "But as a total stranger. You must promise not to tell anyone who I am."

Remembering what had happened at La Bacheleraie, Brother Mathurin's heart sank. If Father De Montfort went to the busy Dominican convent as a shabbily dressed stranger, there was a good chance that he would not receive the attention he deserved. Perhaps there might even be some trouble about seeing his brother. Whereas with just a few words of explanation. . . .

"No," said Father De Montfort, smiling, for he had read his companion's thoughts. "It's time we had a little more suffering to offer the good Lord. Remember the True Devotion to the Blessed Virgin Mary—*and* the price to be paid so that others may come to know about it?"

"Yes, Father," replied Brother Mathurin resignedly, and said no more. But when they presented themselves at the Dominican church, his worst fears were realized. For after a brief glance in their direction, the friar working in the sacristy paid them no more heed. In fact, he did not even come forward to see what they wanted.

After waiting patiently for several minutes, Father De Montfort took matters into his own hands. "My dear Brother," he said, addressing the sacristan, "might I have permission to offer Mass at the shrine of Blessed Alan?"

An impatient look crossed the white-robed friar's face. "I

"You want someone to serve your Mass, too?"

suppose so!" he snapped, not pausing from his work. And only after considerable delay did he bring forth a set of shabby vestments and two stumps of candles for the use of his visitor.

"You want someone to serve your Mass, too?" he demanded.

Father De Montfort smiled. "No, thank you, Brother. My friend here," indicating Brother Mathurin, "will act as server."

The sacristan shrugged. "All right," he muttered, and continued with his duties.

All through the Mass, Brother Mathurin was troubled and resentful. What was the matter with the sacristan that he should be so abrupt and uncivil? Then after Mass, as Father De Montfort was making his thanksgiving in church, the sacristan motioned Brother Mathurin aside.

"Who's that priest who came with you?" he demanded sharply.

Brother Mathurin hesitated. How could he answer the question without failing in obedience?

"H-he's a very holy man from Poitiers, Brother," he mumbled lamely. "And most devoted to Blessed Alan. In fact, the very reason we're here. . . ."

But the sacristan was no longer listening. *"Brother!"* he exclaimed disdainfully. "You call me that, too? Listen, young man. My rightful title is 'Father,' not 'Brother.'" And at once he launched into an explanation of that custom in the Dominican Order which provides that a priest shall wear an all-white habit, a lay Brother a black scapular over his white tunic.

"I'm a priest," he concluded, pointing to his white scapular. "I say Mass, preach, hear confessions. It's most annoying, as well as incorrect, to call me 'Brother.' Will you kindly explain that to your friend when he's finished with his prayers?"

Taken aback by the friar's irritation, Brother Mathurin nodded humbly. "Of course, Father. And please forgive us! We didn't know about the difference in habits."

The friar's eyes softened. "It's all right," he muttered. "There's no harm done. But . . . well, I guess I'm not in a very good mood today. This work in the sacristy is enough to try the patience of a saint."

"Yes, Father." said Brother Mathurin hastily, "I'm sure it is." And excusing himself as best he could, he hurried back into the church.

CHAPTER 26

A NEW MISSION

FAR from being disturbed over what had happened, Father De Montfort laughed heartily when Brother Mathurin related his private conversation with the sacristan. "So the good soul was put out because we called him 'Brother'?" he mused. "Well, perhaps tomorrow we'll give him another chance to mortify his pride."

Brother Mathurin could scarcely believe his ears. "Father, you don't mean that you're going to call him 'Brother' again!" he burst out.

"Why not?"

"But he'll be terribly angry, Father! He told me especially to be sure and explain. . . . "

"And you did, didn't you? Well, now forget the whole affair."

Poor Brother Mathurin! For the rest of the morning he was restless with anxiety. Surely life held enough troubles without deliberately seeking more? Then that afternoon something else happened. On an errand for Father De Montfort, he came across the Father Sacristan unexpectedly in the street. With a mumbled greeting he sought to hurry past, but the friar caught him by the arm.

"Young man, this morning you forgot to tell me the name of that priest who's traveling with you," he said sternly. "Who is he, anyway? I can't seem to put him out of my mind."

Brother Mathurin squirmed, but this time there was no evading the issue. Finally he blurted out that his companion was Father Louis Mary Grignion, more generally known as Father De Montfort, after his birthplace of Montfort-la-Cane.

"But I wasn't supposed to tell this to anyone!" he stammered. "May God forgive me! What have I done?"

For a moment the sacristan stared. Then, to Brother Mathurin's astonishment, he seized him by the shoulders, "Louis Mary!" he exclaimed excitedly. "And after twenty years! Why, of course he called me 'Brother'! That's just what I am!"

Brother Mathurin hesitated. "Y-you don't mean. . . ."

"Yes, young man, I do mean it. I'm Joseph Peter Grignion. And I've acted like a stupid fool. But Louis Mary will forgive me. I know he will."

The next morning when Father De Montfort arrived at the Dominican church, the Father Sacristan was bubbling over with explanations and apologies. But Father De Montfort brushed them all aside. "Joseph, don't say a word!" he begged, embracing the culprit warmly. "My, how good it is to see you!"

Needless to say, this time a new set of beautiful vestments was laid out for the newcomer, and two fresh candles, Father De Montfort made no comment, but Brother Mathurin felt sure that his flush was one of suppressed laughter.

Of course Father Joseph Peter lost no time in telling his Superior what he had done, and everyone else he met. Within a few days the story was making the rounds of all the religious houses in Dinan, and it was always mentioned that Father De Montfort's missionary powers were quite extraordinary. Soon invitations for him to preach began to pour in from one parish after another, and Father De Montfort gave himself enthusiastically to the unexpected work.

Then came the chance to help out at a mission in one of the larger parishes of Dinan. After this, a retreat to the soldiers at the local garrison; a visit with the Count and Countess de la Garaye (who had recently turned their beautiful home into a shelter for the sick poor), and a mission and retreat in the neighboring towns of Saint-Suliac and Bécherel. Indeed, after some five months of labor, Father De Montfort found himself known and loved throughout the entire countryside. Then, early in the spring of the year 1707, came wonderful news.

"Brother, we've been invited to work with Father Ledeuger in the diocese of Saint-Brieuc," he announced one day. "Oh, how good God is!"

Brother Mathurin looked up curiously. "Father Ledeuger, Father? Why, who is he?"

Father De Montfort could scarcely control his excitement. "One of the most famous missionaries in western France, Brother. When I was just a young priest I thought very seriously about joining him in his work. But my confessor wasn't sure that it would be the best thing for me, and so I put the idea out of my mind. But now—well, God seems to have spoken. We'll be on our way tomorrow."

CHAPTER 27

ORDERED TO LEAVE

A T first all went well in the new mission field. Father
Ledeuger welcomed his new co-workers warmly, and
gave them a number of assignments. In one of these (the
village of La Chèze), Father De Montfort was especially
successful in preaching a mission and restoring a ruined
chapel dedicated to Our Lady of Pity.

Now there was a legend in the neighborhood that two
hundred years before, the great Saint Vincent Ferrer had
wished to restore the chapel but had given up the idea.

"This undertaking is reserved for a man whom the
Almighty will cause to be born in later times," he had said.
"A man who will come as one unknown; a man who will be
greatly contradicted and laughed at; but a man, nevertheless, who will bring this holy enterprise to a happy issue."

Thus, when Father De Montfort set about restoring Our
Lady's chapel, excitement in La Chèze reached fever pitch.
The holy man of Saint Vincent's prophecy had finally arrived! And not only was he restoring Our Lady's chapel.
He was actually living in the village—offering Mass, hearing confessions, preaching and teaching catechism to
young and old alike!

"We must listen to every word he says," the people told
one another eagerly. "He surely is a saint."

But it was not only because he seemed to be fulfilling Saint Vincent Ferrer's prophecy that the countryfolk flocked to Father De Montfort. It was common knowledge that his priestly blessing possessed remarkable powers. Scores of invalids insisted it had cured them of their ailments. Even more. His prayers worked other wonders, too, such as turning a poor crop into a good one, making sick animals well, and bringing peace into troubled households.

Brother Mathurin was delighted at the way things were going. And when, after three months' successful work in Saint-Brieuc it was decided that they should give a mission in Montfort-la-Cane, his joy knew no bounds. Surely there would be even greater success for them in Father De Mont-fort's native town?

True enough. There was great rejoicing in Montfort-la-Cane when it became known that Father De Montfort was about to open a mission. His aged parents, who for some years had been living in Rennes, returned to their old home for the occasion and arranged a joyful celebration in honor of the event.

"Son, we want you to invite all your friends for dinner," his father told him. "It doesn't matter how many you ask. There'll be plenty for everyone."

But soon John Baptist Grignion was regretting his words. For on the day of the dinner not only friends and neighbors were crowding his spacious house and yard but dozens of strangers as well—cripples, beggars and other unfortunates from miles around.

"Well, Father, you did tell me to ask all my friends," said Louis Mary, smiling. "Now, won't there be enough for them?"

"O-of course," said John Baptist, rallying. "Don't worry, son." But as he moved away to attend to details, the old man shook his head in bewilderment. Of all his eighteen children (only eight of whom had lived to maturity), Louis Mary was surely the most unusual. Even as a child he had loved the sick poor with a passionate devotion. Now, a man of thirty-four. . . .

"*All his friends!*" muttered John Baptist, anxious and upset. Then gradually his spirits rose. What had Saint Luke written in his Gospel?

When thou givest a dinner or a supper, do not invite thy friends, or thy brethren, or thy relatives, or thy rich neighbors, lest perhaps they also invite thee in return, and a recompense be made to thee. But when thou givest a feast, invite the poor, the crippled, the lame, the blind; and blessed shalt thou be, because they have nothing to repay thee with; for thou shalt be repaid at the resurrection of the just. . . .

"Those were really the Lord's own words," reflected John Baptist, greatly consoled. "Saint Luke was merely repeating what He said."

However, the crowds at the Grignion house were as nothing to those which presently flocked to the parish church. Brother Mathurin could scarcely conceal his joy as he, with the others, waited for Father De Montfort to mount the pulpit. What a wonderful day this was! Surely much good would come from it?

"Holy Spirit, give Father the right words to say!" he begged silently. "Let him speak as he's never spoken before!"

But Father De Montfort, well realizing that friends and relations were eager to admire his preaching skill and to feel proud of him, had made other plans. Thus, after a fervent prayer before the Tabernacle, he took a large crucifix from a nearby shrine and went up into the pulpit. One minute passed, two minutes, three minutes, and still he was silent, gazing out at the sea of expectant faces raised

John Baptist Grignion was anxious and upset.

to his. Then he calmly fastened the crucifix to the pulpit's edge and without a word came down into the sanctuary.

A gasp ran through the congregation. What had happened? What was wrong? Why had there been no sermon? Was Father De Montfort ill? But no. There he was, kneeling contentedly a few feet away from the pulpit, his eyes full upon the crucifix, his face radiant and at peace. Then presently he arose, and with a smaller crucifix in his hands began to make his way through the hushed crowds.

"Friend, behold Your Saviour," he whispered, presenting the crucifix to be kissed to each one as he passed. "Aren't you sorry for having offended Him?"

The effect was startling. Those who had come to church out of idle curiosity now realized their fault. What sermon was so eloquent as that of the Cross? What priest so holy as the Priest of Priests—Jesus Christ?

So impressive was "The Sermon of the Cross" that the mission at Montfort-la-Cane surpassed all previous ones that had been given there. For several days Father De Montfort was kept busy in the confessional, while Brother Mathurin disposed of hundreds of religious articles at his little stand. Finally, tired but happy, the two returned to Father Ledeuger who was about to open a mission in Moncontour.

It was now August of the year 1707. As he plunged into the work at hand, Father De Montfort's heart filled with joy. He had been associated with Brittany's foremost missionary since early spring, and with God's grace had been able to do much good. Of course he realized that some of his fellow-missionaries looked upon him with disfavor. They did not care to hear so much about the True Devotion to the Blessed Virgin Mary. And many thought he spoke out far too bluntly on the evils of immodest dress and dancing, especially where important and influential people were concerned.

"Still, none of these men is a Jansenist," thought Father De Montfort gratefully. "As for Father Ledeuger—why, he's a real saint."

Then suddenly the blow fell. One afternoon Father Ledeuger sent word for Father De Montfort to come to him at once.

"Father, I must ask you to leave." he declared coldly. "What you did this morning—well, it was just too much for any of us."

Father De Montfort stared in astonishment. "What I did this morning? But . . . but I don't understand!"

The face of the older priest was hard. "Come, come, you're not a child, Father. Didn't you take up a collection after my sermon today—in absolute defiance of all our rules and regulations?"

Father De Montfort's heart sank. That morning Father Ledeuger had preached so eloquently on the duty of having Masses offered for the Souls in Purgatory that afterwards, without stopping to think, he had gone among the congregation seeking alms for this purpose.

"Y-yes, I did take up a collection," he murmured. "But I meant no harm, Father. It was only because. . . . "

Suddenly he stopped. Why should he try to excuse himself? He had been thoughtless. He had broken the rules.

Quietly he knelt down. "You're right, Father," he acknowledged. "I did do wrong. You . . . you really want me to go?"

Unmoved by the humble apology, Father Ledeuger rose to his feet. "That's what I said!" he snapped. "And at once, Father. I'll not stand for disobedience from anyone!"

CHAPTER 28

A NEW COMPANION AND
AN OLD SHRINE

BROTHER Mathurin was beside himself with indignation when he heard what had happened. "Jealousy! That's all it is, Father!" he burst out. "Some of the people here can't bear to see how much good you do. Why, Father Ledeuger was just looking for an excuse. . . . "

"Brother!" exclaimed Father De Montfort in horrified tones. "That's no way to talk about a holy priest!"

"It's true, though," muttered Brother Mathurin stubbornly. "You're the best preacher in the whole mission band, Father. Why, in the last six months you've made more conversions than anyone else! Don't you suppose some of the other missionaries here resent that—especially when you're younger and less experienced than they are?"

But Father De Montfort would not listen to such talk. What had happened was God's Will. They would leave Moncontour at once and return to Montfort-la-Cane. Outside the town there was an abandoned house near a chapel dedicated to Saint Lazarus. Surely permission could be secured to live here for a while as hermits?

"Preaching is a good work, Brother, but one must have something worthwhile to say," explained Father De Montfort. "If we spend ourselves in prayer for a change, rather than in action, I'm sure the Holy Spirit will refresh our minds, and we'll be able to do so much more for people when we take up missionary work again."

Brother Mathurin sighed. "Yes, Father," he murmured resignedly. "I suppose so."

But as they set out for Montfort-la-Cane, an encouraging thing happened. A young man named John approached Father De Montfort and asked permission to travel with him. Even more. He wanted to be a Brother, too, if that was at all possible.

Father De Montfort looked at him curiously. He was a country lad, slightly older than Brother Mathurin, shabbily dressed and without much education. But he had an honest face.

"Son, what makes you think you'd like to be one of us?" he asked kindly. "We're only poor missionaries, you know, without even a home of our own. If you come with us, you can expect very little in the way of comfort."

John shrugged. "That's all right, Father. I've heard you preach many times. And what you had to say about Our Lady—well, it set me to thinking. I'd like nothing better than to help you to make her better known—if I may."

Father De Montfort was silent. John seemed to be a good young man—healthy, devout, eager. Undoubtedly he would be useful in many ways. But what a pity he was not a priest! Then the Company of Mary would really become a reality. Yet after a moment he put aside his disappointment. In God's own time priest-helpers would come. Just now it was surely His Will that two lay Brothers be his sole companions?

"Very well, John, you may join us," he said finally. "Go ahead with Brother Mathurin. He'll explain about our work."

Brother Mathurin was only too happy to oblige. But he

did not paint a cheerful picture of the future. Father De Montfort was a saint, he said. And one of the finest preachers in France. But what enemies he had, especially among the Jansenists! No matter how successful his missions and retreats, there was always some kind of trouble afterwards. Thus, just now Father Ledeuger had ordered them to leave Moncontour. Eighteen months ago the Bishop of Poitiers had banished them from his diocese. As a result, Sister Mary Louise was now alone at the poorhouse, with no young girls willing to join her in her work.

"Sister Mary Louise?" repeated Brother John curiously. "Why, who is she?"

Brother Mathurin hastened to give an account of Father De Montfort's work in Poitiers; his meeting with Mary Louise Trichet; his hope of founding a community of women religious who would work among the sick poor and, like his missionary priests and Brothers-to-be, spread the True Devotion to the Blessed Virgin Mary. But so far things had not turned out well. No priests had come to join them. And Sister Mary Louise had found no companion, either.

"Father De Montfort prays for her every day, though," concluded Brother Mathurin. "And he also prays for another young woman in Poitiers—Catherine Brunet. You see, he's quite sure that God is calling Catherine to be the second Daughter of Wisdom, but the last time he talked with her she just laughed at the idea."

Brother John listened with interest to all that Brother Mathurin had to say. But he was especially touched by the story of Sister Mary Louise. To think that she had promised to remain alone at the poorhouse in Poitiers for ten years, leading the life of a religious while deprived of so many of its consolations!

"I'm going to pray for her, too," he decided. "She surely needs to be remembered."

Brother John was as good as his word, and in the next few weeks offered many a prayer for Sister Mary Louise. And he offered work, too. For although Father De Montfort, Brother Mathurin and he were now hermits in the wooded hills above Montfort-la-Cane, some days they spent almost as much time in manual labor as they did in prayer. The reason? Their present headquarters, the house and chapel dedicated to Saint Lazarus, had been neglected for years, and they had decided to restore them.

"We'll rededicate the chapel to Our Lady," Father De Montfort promised. "It'll make a beautiful place of pilgrimage for the people of Montfort-la-Cane."

Naturally the whole countryside was delighted that Father De Montfort had returned, and crowds came to help him with his work. In fact, by the end of October no one would have recognized the little chapel that had been in ruins for so long. Now a beautiful statue of Our Lady of Wisdom stood in the sanctuary, while outside the railing was a handsome kneeling-desk. Attached to this was a wooden rosary with beads as large as walnuts, and of such a length that several people could use it at the same time.

Father De Montfort was overjoyed at all that had been done. Surely the shrine of Our Lady of Wisdom, looking out on the picturesque landscape of river, forest and rocky valley, was one of the most blessed places in the whole world?

"Dearest Mother, please let much good come from this little shrine," he begged. "Grant your choicest gifts to all who journey here in your honor."

His prayer was answered. All through the winter of 1707 and well into the spring of 1708, pilgrims flocked to the woodland chapel of Our Lady of Wisdom in the peaceful hills above Montfort-la-Cane. Frequently Father De Montfort spoke to these visitors on the enormous power of the Rosary to win graces for themselves and others. Also on the True Devotion to the Blessed Virgin Mary—that much misunderstood Act of Consecration by which a person gives himself into Our Lady's hands to become the slave of Jesus, just as she once was, and so win Heaven with far less trouble than by his own poor efforts.

"Friends, it's such an easy thing to make the Act of Consecration," he repeatedly told his audience. "Even a child can say, and mean, these simple words: *I am all Thine and all I have is Thine, O most loving Jesus, through Mary, Thy holy Mother.*' But the results? Oh, I just can't describe what the Holy Slavery does for souls, especially the souls of the weak, the suffering, the tempted!"

Such talks bore good fruit. Frequently Father De Montfort was asked to leave his hermitage to preach in Montfortla-Cane and other neighboring towns, with the result that the Rosary and the True Devotion to the Blessed Virgin Mary became known and loved by all.

But of course the Jansenists were not idle. Indeed, they were quite put out about such success, and one day a group of them sought out the Bishop of Saint-Malo, in whose diocese Montfort-la-Cane was situated.

"Your Lordship, something's got to be done about this upstart priest," they insisted. "Why, he's disturbing the peace of the whole countryside!" Then, to make their grievance sound more plausible, they declared that people were deserting their parish churches for services at Father De Montfort's hermitage. Money that rightfully belonged to local pastors was falling into his hands.

Unfortunately the Bishop lent a ready ear to these stories. "Why, this is a disgrace!" he said angrily. "I'll go to Montfort-la-Cane at once and put a stop to such abuse."

CHAPTER 29

WHERE TO DIG?

THE Bishop did go to Montfort-la-Cane. And though
Father De Montfort's friends stood by him loyally, it
was his enemies who won the day. There were to be no
more public gatherings at the chapel of Our Lady of
Wisdom, said the Bishop. If Father De Montfort wished to
preach or to hear confessions, he must do so in some
parish church.

Of course Brothers Mathurin and John were disappointed. How hard they had worked to restore Our Lady's
chapel! And how the people had loved to come there on pilgrimage! Now, if there were to be no more services. . . .

"Let's not worry about anything," said Father De Montfort consolingly. "The Bishop is our lawful superior. We're
pleasing God and Our Lady if we do just what he says."

But as the days passed, Father De Montfort gradually
became convinced that the time was fast approaching for
him and his companions to leave their hermit life. It was
only too clear that the Bishop of Saint-Malo did not
approve of the True Devotion to the Blessed Virgin Mary.
Although he had not actually forbidden it to be preached,
he might do so at any moment. Whereas in some other diocese where the authorities were more friendly. . . .

"Brothers, I think we'd better go to Nantes," he announced one day. "Something tells me that there is work for us there."

So in May of 1708, not without regrets, the three said farewell to the little hermitage and chapel in the wooded hills above Montfort-la-Cane and set out for Nantes. To their great joy they were warmly received, especially by the Vicar General, and soon Father De Montfort was busy with the missionary work he loved so much. A Jesuit priest, one Father Joubert, was assigned to help him with his first mission at Saint-Similien, a suburb of the city. Then a second priest, Father des Bastières, joined him for a few months. By Christmas time there had been missions and retreats in dozens of parishes, with splendid results.

But it was in April of 1709 that Father De Montfort received his most important assignment. This was a mission at Pontchâteau, some thirty miles from Nantes. So many graces manifested themselves during the three weeks he spent there that he decided to leave behind him some kind of memorial.

But what would it be? Then presently his thoughts went back to the winter of 1703 when the Cardinal Archbishop of Paris had sent him to restore peace to the hermits of Mont Valérien. How often he had admired the beautiful Calvary outside the hermits' monastery! How easy it had been to pray in that holy place, one's eyes upon the crosses and statues which recalled the sufferings and death of Jesus! Now, if only something similar could be erected at Pontchâteau . . . even one cross bearing a figure of the dead Christ . . .

"That's it," he decided. "I'll build a simple Calvary here in remembrance of the mission."

When priests and people heard about the plan, they were full of enthusiasm. Everyone promised to help build the Calvary, and after some delay a promising site was chosen outside the town.

"We'll dig a circular trench, take the earth from this and pile it in the center," explained Father De Montfort. "That will make a kind of hill. On top of the hill we'll put the cross."

So it was agreed, and at once several men set to work digging the trench. But after two or three days, doubts arose in Father De Montfort's mind. Was the site for the new Calvary really the best? Wouldn't it be more appropriate to have it built nearer the town, and on a natural hilltop?

"Friends, let's pray about the matter before we go any farther," he suggested. "You know, it may be that God would rather have the Calvary somewhere else."

So work came to a halt, and that night Father De Montfort retired to a nearby chapel to pray for guidance. In the morning, when the men arrived to resume their labors, he took them into the chapel and asked them to pray, too. Then presently everyone came outside. And to the astonishment of all, two white doves were seen to descend upon the place of excavation, fill their beaks with earth, and fly swiftly away. At least ten times the wonder was repeated, after which the birds were seen no more.

"What does it mean, Father?" inquired Brother Mathurin excitedly. "Where do you suppose the doves took that earth?"

Father De Montfort shook his head. "I don't know, Brother. But maybe we can find out. After all, they couldn't have gone far."

True enough. During a short walk through the open fields, Father De Montfort and his friends came upon an amazing sight—the doves, happily cooing and strangely tame—were nestling beside a little hive-shaped mound of fresh earth! Even more. The spot was the top of a beautiful hill not far from Pontchâteau, with an impressive view of the country for miles around.

"Friends, this is where we build!"

Suddenly all was clear to Father De Montfort. His nightlong vigil in the little chapel and the workmen's prayers had been blessed by God! The doves were really messengers from Heaven, sent to show the site of the new Calvary. . . .

"Friends, this is it!" he exclaimed joyfully. "This is where we build!"

Even as the people gathered about excitedly, a host of new ideas filled Father De Montfort's mind. Previously he had thought to build only a simple Calvary—a single cross. But now the Calvary of Pontchâteau must be the largest and most impressive in all France, on an even greater scale than that at Mont Valérien. Atop this present hill would be another hill—a giant, man-made summit with three crosses bearing full-size figures of Christ and the two thieves. Standing at the foot of the center cross would be Our Lady, Saint John and Saint Mary Magdalen. And on the winding path leading up to the crosses would be lifelike representations of the apostles and disciples, the Roman soldiers and the Jewish leaders who had persecuted the Saviour. In other words, the Calvary of Pontchâteau would duplicate the Calvary of Jerusalem in as much detail as possible.

"What a wonderful idea, Father!" cried Brother John when he heard the news. "When do we start working?"

Father De Montfort smiled. "When, Brother? Why, right away, of course. This very minute."

CHAPTER 30

THE CALVARY AT PONTCHÂTEAU

BY sunset of that same day three large circles, one inside the other, had been traced about the spot wherethe doves had come to rest, and the digging of trenches begun. At the end of the week the earth taken from these had mounted steadily within the smallest circle as the people of Pontchâteau gave themselves to the arduous task of raising a seventy-foot mound for the new Calvary.

"Even the women and children are helping," observed Brother Mathurin in astonishment, gazing at the extraordinary sight of four hundred persons, with pick and shovel and wheelbarrow, going about their assigned tasks in prayerful silence. "Oh, Father! I never saw anything like this in my whole life!"

"Neither did I," confessed Father De Montfort. "But do you know something, Brother? I think it's only the beginning. God, in His goodness, is going to send us still more helpers."

Father De Montfort was right. As word spread of what was happening at Pontchâteau, people flocked from neighboring towns to volunteer their services. Thus, there was never a lack of workers. For when one person laid down his tools to see to duties at home, another was ready to take his place. And strangely enough, no one found the labor tiresome or difficult. Buoyed up by a mysterious energy, even young girls shoveled and dug and carried heavy baskets of earth without strain.

Even more amazing—there was no disorder of any kind. All prayed as they worked, and during the regular rest periods Father De Montfort led the workers in singing hymns or gave them an encouraging talk. Then, too, from time to time he announced new plans for the Calvary. For instance, not only was there to be the man-made hill with its giant crosses and statues. About the base of the Calvary—the largest circle he had traced on the first day of work—one hundred and fifty fir trees were to be planted, representing the one hundred and fifty Hail Marys of the Rosary, with a cypress tree between each ten firs to represent the fifteen Our Fathers. There would also be two small gardens at the Calvary entrance, and several chapels along the winding path leading up to the Crucifixion scene.

"All this will take months of work, but if it gives glory to God and helps us to pray more fruitfully, it's well worthwhile," he declared.

Since everything was so thoroughly organized, Father De Montfort presently decided that he could safely leave Pontchâteau and continue with his missionary work elsewhere. Accompanied by a priest-volunteer, one Father Olivier, he accordingly set out for the neighboring town of Missilac. Here he preached a most fruitful mission and also arranged for a fifty-foot chestnut tree to be cut down and dragged to Pontchâteau by twelve yoke of oxen. This would furnish the wood for the three crosses.

Soon there were other missions—at Herbignac, Camoël, Saint-Donatien, Bouguenais—interrupted by frequent visits to Pontchâteau to see how things were going. There were also visits to Nantes, where the statues and furnishings for the chapels were being made. And, of course, in each of these places new workers were recruited. Indeed, when a year had passed, word of what was taking place at Pontchâteau had spread throughout all France, and even to Holland and Spain. Scores of pilgrims from far-away places arrived each week, eager to have a hand in building the gigantic Calvary. Nor were they all simple peasant folk. Many were possessed of considerable means, and it was no uncommon sight to see fashionably dressed men and women descend from their luxurious carriages, take up a pick and shovel, and set to work.

"I can hardly believe my eyes," declared Brother Mathurin over and over again.

"It's almost too good to be true," said Brother John.

As for Brother Nicholas, a new recruit to their ranks, he was in a state of constant excitement. "I can't get over it!" he kept exclaiming. "The work never seems to tire anyone, not even the noble ladies! Is it a miracle?"

"Of course," said Father De Montfort, smiling. "God is very good to us, Brother. He's blessing our labors in a wonderful way."

Finally the Calvary was finished—in August of 1710. As he gazed upon the fruit of fifteen months of toil, Father De Montfort's heart filled with joy. What a glorious memorial to the mission he had given in Pontchâteau! Why, the giant crosses and statues could be seen for miles around! Then, how beautiful were the little chapels dotting the landscaped terraces, the gardens and flowers! *And* the eighty-foot rosary, stretched high around the summit of the Calvary! Surely no one could visit such a representation of the Lord's suffering and death without obtaining the choicest of blessings?

"It's the finest Calvary in all France, Father," insisted Brother Mathurin with righteous pride. "I just know it's going to do enormous good."

Everyone else was of the same opinion, and there was scarcely an hour of the day when pilgrims were not climbing the winding path to the Crucifixion scene, meditating in the chapels, or making their way around the picturesque rosary of fir and cypress trees circling the base of the Calvary. And when it was announced that there would be a solemn dedication service on September 14, the Feast of the Exaltation of the Holy Cross, there was even greater excitement. Indeed, Brothers Mathurin, John and Nicholas could scarcely contain themselves. What a wonderful day the fourteenth was going to be! Besides the solemn blessing of the Calvary by Father De Montfort, there would be sermons by four different priests, a procession with candles and banners and hymn singing, the recitation of the Rosary and the public renewal of Baptismal vows. As for crowds—certainly Pontchâteau would never have seen the like.

"There ought to be ten thousand people here anyway," ventured Brother Nicholas hopefully.

"Ten thousand? Why, there'll be twice that number!" exclaimed Brother John.

Brother Mathurin was silent. For five long years he had been working with Father De Montfort—years filled with troubles and misunderstandings of all kinds. But now the hour of triumph was at hand. The beautiful Calvary of Pontchâteau was finished. And in a little while the man who had made everything possible. . . .

"Yes, the fourteenth will be a wonderful day," he agreed thoughtfully. "God be praised!"

CHAPTER 31

THE BOMBSHELL

ON the thirteenth of September it seemed that every road in France must lead to Pontchâteau. Hundreds of peasants, eager to obtain a good place for the next day's celebration, had begun massing about the Calvary at the first light of dawn. Some had come on foot, others in carts drawn by oxen or mules. Soon more hundreds had arrived, including John Baptist Grignion and his family from Rennes. A number of the nobility were also on hand, their rich garments in striking contrast to the simple homespun of the countryfolk. Then in the late afternoon came an urgent message from the Bishop of Nantes.

"His Lordship must be on the way, too!" exclaimed Brother Nicholas happily, as he and his companions came running to learn the contents of the letter. "What an honor for us all!"

"Maybe he's decided to bless the Calvary himself," suggested Brother John. "Won't that be wonderful?"

But Brother Mathurin, closely observing Father De Montfort as he scanned the Bishop's message, felt a sinking of heart. Surely there was no good news in the letter!

"W-what is it, Father?" he burst out. "What's wrong?"

A peculiar expression crossed Father De Montfort's face. Then he smiled faintly at his anxious follower. "Nothing,

Brother, except that the Bishop doesn't want me to bless
the Calvary tomorrow."

It was as though a bombshell had fallen. The Calvary
was not to be blessed? The thousands of pilgrims had come
to Pontchâteau in vain?

"Father, it can't be!" protested Brother Nicholas. "How
could the Bishop issue such an order? Why, our Calvary is
positively beautiful. . . . "

But Brothers Mathurin and John, more experienced
than their companion, looked at each other in horrified
silence. The Jansenists again! Somehow or other they had
influenced the Bishop to withdraw his approval at the last
moment, and now tomorrow's great celebration must be
canceled!

"Father, it's not fair!"

"It's a crime, Father! That's what it is!"

"Oh, those wretched enemies of ours!"

But Father De Montfort was not listening. With surprising calmness he announced that he would leave at
once for Nantes. Yes, it was a thirty-mile trip, and he
would have to walk all night in order to reach the Bishop's
house, but with God's help he would do just that.
Somehow or other he would make the Bishop realize the
importance of tomorrow's blessing. Then he would hurry
back to Pontchâteau in time for the scheduled celebration
the next afternoon.

"But you can't make a sixty-mile trip in twenty-four
hours, Father!" exclaimed Brother Mathurin, almost in
tears. "You know you can't!"

Father De Montfort smiled. "Why not, Brother? Hasn't
Our Lady often arranged difficult things for me before?"

But at six o'clock the next morning, Father De Montfort
knew that the trip to Nantes had been useless. The
Jansenists had so poisoned the Bishop's mind that nothing could induce him to approve of the new Calvary. He

It was the most beautiful Calvary in France

was soon on his return journey and reached Pontchâteau
late that same night. Then to his joyful relief he found
that the afternoon had not been without a celebration
after all. Two of the four preachers had spoken from the
Calvary. Twenty thousand people had sung hymns,
marched in procession, recited the Rosary and renewed
their Baptismal vows. And alms for the new Calvary had
been most generous.

"Yet things weren't at all what they might have been if
you'd been here, Father," said Brother Mathurin disconsolately. "And the lies and gossip about you! Oh, they're
almost too much to bear!"

Poor Brother Mathurin! The worst blow was yet to
come. A few days later, while Father De Montfort was
preaching a mission at the nearby village of Saint-Molf,
word came from the Bishop that the work was to be
turned over to another priest. No longer had Brittany's
foremost missionary permission to preach and hear confessions in the diocese of Nantes. Even worse. The Calvary
which he had caused to be built must be completely
destroyed at once.

"Dear God!" groaned Brother Mathurin, scarcely able to
believe his ears, "This is the end of everything! What are
we going to do now?"

The people of Pontchâteau were dumbfounded. Their
beautiful Calvary was to be destroyed? Fifteen months of
hard work for nothing?

"It *can't* be true!" they protested. "The Bishop just does-
n't understand!"

"Of course not. Why, he's never even seen our Calvary!"

"Maybe if we explained things to him. . . ."

But the Bishop was in no mood to listen to explanations.
By now not only the Jansenists but important members of
the Government had led him to believe that Father De
Montfort was a dangerous man. In fact, he might even be

a British spy, and the Calvary a camouflaged fortress. If the British (with whom the French were then at war) should land in Brittany, they would undoubtedly find vast quantities of weapons and ammunition hidden beneath the chapels and crosses.

"The Calvary must be destroyed for the sake of public safety," repeated the Bishop sternly. "Those are my orders from Paris."

Father De Montfort bore the new campaign of lies and slander with his customary patience. He withdrew from public life, and for two weeks remained in complete retirement with the Jesuits in Nantes. Then, in October, he was once again seen in the streets of the city. But not as a celebrated missionary, going from one church to another to preach, hear confessions, teach catechism. Now the only priestly privilege allowed him was the private celebration of Holy Mass.

"Father, surely something can be done about your case!" protested Brothers Mathurin, John and Nicholas. "The Jansenists are out to ruin everything for you, but you still have thousands of friends. If only all these would get together somehow. . . . "

But Father De Montfort shook his head. "The Bishop is our lawful superior," he said gently. "As long as we stay in Nantes, we must do what he says."

The Brothers looked at one another silently. There was no arguing this point. But why did they have to stay in Nantes—misunderstood, humiliated, rejected by everyone in authority? Surely it was foolish for such a brilliant man as Father De Montfort to live almost like a layman? To spend his days in visiting the poor and sick, his nights in prayer and penance for those who persecuted him, when he could do so much good as a missionary in some other diocese where the Bishop was more friendly?

Then presently Father De Montfort made a startling

announcement. On November 10, he said—just a few days hence—he was going to join the Dominican Order.

Brother Mathurin turned pale. His beloved superior was entering a convent of Friars Preachers? Why, what would become of Brothers John, Nicholas and himself? *And* Sister Mary Louise?

"Father, you don't mean it!" he burst out. "You're not going to leave us alone!"

Father De Montfort smiled. "Of course not. I'll still be with you, Brother."

"But . . . but you said. . . . "

"I know. But I'm joining Saint Dominic's family as a Tertiary. Surely you understand what that means?"

Brother Mathurin hesitated. Then he shook his head forlornly. "A Tertiary? No, Father. I haven't the slightest idea."

CHAPTER 32

MISSION TO THE CALVINISTS

FATHER De Montfort proceeded to explain about Dominican Tertiaries. They were men and women from all walks of life, he said, who had become members of Saint Dominic's family while still carrying on their duties in the world. By offering certain extra prayers and sacrifices each day, wearing a small white woolen scapular under their ordinary clothes and cultivating an interest in the special aims of the Order, they were also Saint Dominic's children and shared in all the prayers and good works of the preaching friars and cloistered nuns. Of course a similar privilege was granted by certain other religious groups, too—such as the Franciscans, the Augustinians, the Servites, the Carmelites, the Minims, the Norbertines and the Benedictines. Each of these, with its special mission in the Church, had a place for zealous lay-folk.

"But the Third Order of Saint Dominic appeals to me the most," confessed Father De Montfort. "Can you guess why?"

"No, Father," said Brother Mathurin, still somewhat at sea but immeasurably relieved that he was not going to lose his beloved superior. "Unless it's because your brother in Dinan is a Dominican friar?"

"No," said Father De Montfort, smiling. "That's not the reason."

"I know!" burst out Brother John suddenly. "It's because of the Blessed Virgin, isn't it, Father? *And* the Rosary! Saint Dominic was so devoted to them both! Then, he was a great preacher, too, especially against the heretics, and in many ways a lot of your problems are just like his."

Father De Montfort nodded with satisfaction. "Yes, that's it," he admitted. "For a long time—in fact, ever since I went to Rome—I've been feeling the need to belong to Saint Dominic in a special way. You see, something keeps telling me that as a Tertiary—a member of his Third Order for people living in the world—what I've been trying to do for souls will be far more blessed by God."

Brother Nicholas looked up with sudden interest. "You mean you won't have any more troubles?"

Father De Montfort laughed heartily. "No, I couldn't promise that, Brother. What I mean is that once I become a Tertiary, I'll have a special share in the prayers and sacrifices of the friars and nuns of Saint Dominic's family. Then, how much harder for the Devil to keep me from doing good work and getting to heaven than if I were all by myself!"

This and other discussions of Dominican Tertiary life set the Brothers' minds at rest; and when, on November 10, 1710, Father De Montfort was received into the Third Order by the Dominican friars in Nantes, they derived considerable pleasure from the event. Surely from now on the work he was trying to do would be more specially blessed by God?

At first, however, there was no visible indication of this. The Bishop still insisted that Father De Montfort refrain from preaching, teaching or hearing confessions. He might offer Mass privately and help certain devout people who were trying to establish a hospital for incurables, but no more.

When, in the spring of 1711, the Loire River overflowed and a great part of Nantes was under water, Father De

Montfort exhibited heroic courage. Under his direction a number of men took their boats, laden with provisions, into the flooded sections of the town. The risks of the expedition were very great. Several times the boats in the little fleet narrowly escaped capsizing as they made their way through the treacherous currents swirling about the housetops, past floating trees and melting ice, to deliver their precious cargo through upper story windows and even down chimneys. But the venture succeeded, and everywhere Father De Montfort was acclaimed a hero.

Still the Bishop would not relent. "Hero or not, he's a troublemaker," he declared, unable to forget the malicious stories which had been poured into his ears. "He'll not have any rights in my diocese."

Despite his genuine humility, Father De Montfort did not find it easy to be persecuted and misunderstood. Then, too, what a cross to know that even now the beautiful Calvary of Pontchâteau was being relentlessly leveled to the ground! Yet surely some day it would rise again, more beautiful than ever. Surely some day the present suffering would bring forth fruit a hundredfold.

Then, wholly unexpectedly, came wonderful news. Two Bishops invited Father De Montfort to leave Nantes for work in their dioceses. One was the Most Reverend John de Lescure, Bishop of Luçon; the other, the Most Reverend Stephen de Champflour, Bishop of La Rochelle.

"Thank God!" cried Brother Mathurin when he heard the news. "I couldn't have stood this much longer, Father."

Brothers John and Nicholas were jubilant. "The prayers and good works of Saint Dominic's friars and nuns are beginning to bear fruit," they insisted.

Father De Montfort was grateful for the chance to leave Nantes, but he lost no time in explaining that the future would not be without its trials. For instance, the Bishops of Luçon and La Rochelle were good and holy men, and

Jansenism was nowhere as strong in their dioceses as it was in Poitiers, Saint-Malo or Nantes. But another evil, Calvinism, was very firmly entrenched, and that was why the two Bishops were so eager to have missions and retreats for the people.

"Now, what do you know about Calvinism, Brothers?" asked Father De Montfort earnestly.

The three hesitated, then shook their heads. "Nothing," they admitted. "What is it, Father?"

Eager to prepare his helpers for the difficult tasks ahead, Father De Montfort presently began the story of John Calvin, the French heretic who had died in 1564, and who had done such harm to souls by his doctrine of predestination—the belief that God does not will the salvation of all men but only of a select few.

"Calvin insisted that man has no free will, and that it's impossible for certain people to avoid going to hell because they can't help doing wrong," he explained. "He also denied the doctrine of the Real Presence."

"You mean the Calvinists don't believe in the Blessed Sacrament?" exclaimed Brother Nicholas in shocked tones.

"They'd like nothing better than to empty every Tabernacle in the world," declared Father De Montfort. Then, as the three stood looking at him in horror, he smiled.

"Let's not worry too much about the Calvinists, though. With Our Lady's help—and Saint Dominic's—we'll be able to make friends of many of these poor people. Why, it could well happen. . . . "

"What could, Father?"

"That we'll do the best work of our lives in the dioceses of Luçon and La Rochelle. Perhaps in one or the other the Company of Mary will soon become a reality. And the Daughters of Wisdom, too."

The Brothers looked at one another with renewed courage. How wonderful if Father De Montfort's words proved true!

CHAPTER 33

VERDICT OF THE THREE CANONS

IN March of that same year, 1711, Father De Montfort left Nantes for a mission in La Garnache, a little town in the diocese of Luçon. This was a great success, and was followed by other work in the city of Luçon. Then in May he set out for La Rochelle, where Bishop de Champflour had arranged for him to preach in the suburb of Lhoumeau. If all went well here, there would be several other missions in La Rochelle itself.

As usual, vast crowds came to hear Father De Montfort speak, and there were hundreds of conversions. Never had there been such a mission as at Lhoumeau, people said. In the pulpit Father De Montfort was like a thundering prophet from the pages of the Old Testament. Hardened sinners wept openly over their misdeeds. But in the confessional—ah, what a difference! Here he was gentleness itself—fatherly, sympathetic, kind. No one went away unconsoled, or without feeling that he had made a real friend.

Of course the Calvinists were beside themselves at such success, especially when they discovered that several from their own ranks had attended the mission at Lhoumeau and become converted to the Catholic Church. When the first of the city missions began, they did their best to stir up trouble. Some went so far as to waylay Father De Montfort in the street, spit in his face and beat him with sticks and stones. There were even plots against his life. As a result, several of the local clergy became worried. Perhaps it would be better if Father De Montfort were to stop preaching and leave La Rochelle at once. After all, there had been serious trouble in other places where he had worked. And no one could deny that his missionary methods were most unusual. For instance, so many processions with lighted candles, banners, hymn singing, public Acts of Contrition! Then, all this talk about becoming a saint easily and quickly through the True Devotion to the Blessed Virgin Mary. . . .

"He works the idea into almost every sermon he gives," they told the Bishop. "And that's hardly prudent, Your Lordship."

Bishop de Champflour was a patient man. He listened carefully to his worried visitors, but refrained from giving any opinion of his own. In fact, as the bitterness and resentment against Father De Montfort increased in both Protestant and Catholic circles, he experienced a strange sense of satisfaction.

"All hell seems to be breaking loose here in La Rochelle," he reflected. "Maybe that's so heaven can have a chance."

In the end he enlisted the services of three learned canons of the Cathedral. They were to observe Father De Montfort closely, attend all his mission services and report in detail everything that took place.

"I'm especially interested in learning more about the True Devotion to the Blessed Virgin Mary," he said. "What is there about this doctrine that appeals so much to some people and yet causes others such great distress—even the very holiest priests and religious?"

The three canons promised they would attend the mission services—separately and inconspicuously, as the

Bishop suggested—and make notes at all the sermons. They would also pray for light to render an honest report on Father De Montfort's work. True, the first mission at the General Hospital was about over. But three others were scheduled to open in the near future—for men, women and soldiers, respectively—at the Dominican church. Undoubtedly Father De Montfort would soon be repeating his disturbing doctrines.

Within a few weeks the canons returned to the Bishop's house, armed with sheafs of notes. The mission for men was almost over, they said, and they were ready to make their first report.

"Well, what do you think of Father De Montfort?" asked the Bishop eagerly. "Is he preaching heresy? Is he a tool of the Devil, as some people say? *Or* a madman?"

The canons had but one answer for the three questions. "He's a saint, Your Lordship. We've heard nothing at his men's mission that wasn't true, inspiring, beautiful, good."

The Bishop gave a sigh of relief. "And the True Devotion—what about that?"

The canons looked at one another in silence. Then the oldest spoke out abruptly. "If everyone were to understand and practice the True Devotion to the Blessed Virgin Mary, Your Lordship, the world would be a place of thoroughly happy and holy souls."

For a moment the Bishop was thoughtful. "Then why is there so much talk against it?" he demanded. "Why so much fussing and fuming, even on the part of good people?"

The second canon shrugged. "Because it's so simple, Your Lordship."

"Simple?"

"Yes. Didn't you know that very many good people are suspicious of simple things? They've grown up to think that the only way to go to heaven is the hard way—by their own struggles, their own prayers, their own sacrifices.* Deep down in their hearts they have too much pride to admit that they and all they do are really nothing in God's sight."

"But surely. . . ."

The first canon nodded emphatically. "It's true, Your Lordship. It takes a great deal of humility to practice the True Devotion. In my opinion, that's why sinners appreciate it much more readily than good people. They know they've fallen from grace; that they deserve to go to hell a thousand times; that, barring a miracle, they'll probably fall again, no matter how many prayers and sacrifices they offer to God. So, in a sense, they stop struggling. They give themselves to Our Lady as slaves of her Son, and ask her to make them into what they ought to be."

The Bishop smiled. "I know many holy people who'd consider that the lazy, even the cowardly thing to do," he said. "But never mind them. Tell me more about Father De Montfort's True Devotion to the Blessed Virgin Mary."

The canons did their best to obey, first one and then another quoting from his notes and repeating passages from Father De Montfort's sermons. All agreed that, on first hearing, the words "slave" and "slavery" were frightening and repulsive. Yet surely the word "love" changed everything? "A slave of love" was not a phrase to disturb anyone.

"And that's what a person is who practices the True Devotion, Your Lordship. He makes the Act of Consecration to Our Lady, not because he *has* to but because he *wants* to. He gives her everything—himself, his possessions, the satisfactory merit of his prayers and works— just as Saint Bernard advises."

The Bishop looked up with interest. "Saint Bernard? But he lived six centuries ago! What has he got to do with

---

*See Note on page 91.

"Father De Montfort's a saint, Your Lordship."

the True Devotion?"

"A great deal, Your Lordship, because his whole life was one long Act of Consecration to Our Lady. Father De Montfort often quotes one of his favorite sayings: 'If you wish to present something to God, no matter how small it may be, place it in Mary's hands if you do not wish to be refused.'"

"That's right. It's as though a poor man, owing rent for his farm to a king, has nothing to give at the end of the year but a worm-eaten apple. If he were wise, and well liked by the queen, wouldn't he give the apple to her? Then she, out of kindness to the poor man, as also out of respect for the king, would remove the spoiled part from the apple, place it on a gold dish and surround it with flowers. Would the king be able to refuse such a gift then? Of course not. He'd receive it gratefully from the hands of the queen who so favored the poor man."

"Yes, Your Lordship. And in one sense we're all like that poor farmer. We owe God so much! But what have we to give Him? After all—unless we're too proud to admit it— our very best prayers and sacrifices are less than dust and ashes in His sight because of our sins."

On and on went the canons with their explanations and comments on the True Devotion to the Blessed Virgin Mary. It was something most praiseworthy, they said. Everyone could practice it, even small children, for the entire substance was contained in a few simple words: *"I am all Thine and all that I have is Thine, O most loving Jesus, through Mary, Thy holy Mother."*

The Bishop smiled with relief. How splendid to hear such an encouraging report from these learned priests! To know that Father De Montfort was preaching something so beautiful and good in the diocese of La Rochelle!

"That little prayer you just said—it's the short form of the Act of Consecration, isn't it?" he asked.

The canons nodded. "Yes, Your Lordship. It's supposed to be said at least once a day by those who practice the True Devotion—preferably in the morning."

For a moment the Bishop was thoughtful. Then he leaned forward eagerly. "I don't suppose. . . . "

"Yes, Your Lordship?"

"I don't suppose you could give me the regular form of the Act of Consecration?"

There was some hesitation as the three canons consulted their notes. Then one produced a sheet of paper. "The Act itself is rather long, Your Lordship, but here's the most important passage. Shall I read it?"

The Bishop settled back in his chair. "Yes," he said. "And slowly and carefully, please. I want to follow every word."

So without delay and with evident relish the canon began to read Father De Montfort's famous offering which · for years the Devil had been trying to keep from the knowledge of men:

In the presence of the heavenly court I choose thee this day for my Mother and mistress, I deliver and consecrate to thee, as thy slave, my body and soul, my goods, both interior and exterior, and even the value of all my good actions, past, present and future; leaving to thee the entire and full right of disposing of me, and all that belongs to me, without exception, according to thy good pleasure, for the greater glory of God, in time and eternity. . . .

CHAPTER 34

PIRATES!

SO impressed was the Bishop by the possibilities for good in Father De Montfort's True Devotion to the Blessed Virgin Mary that he lost no time in assuring him of his complete approval and support. No matter what the Calvinists did or said, he was to continue giving missions in La Rochelle.

"The next one will be for women, won't it, Father?" he inquired kindly.

Father De Montfort nodded, grateful beyond words for the Bishop's trust and confidence. "Yes, Your Lordship. And after that, there'll be the one for soldiers."

However, the Calvinists were not easily discouraged. So, for once Father De Montfort stood in well with a Bishop, did he? He had permission to preach, hear confessions, teach catechism, organize religious processions?

"We'll see about that," they told one another angrily. "If lies and gossip won't turn the trick, we'll get rid of this wretched priest in some other way."

Fortunately Father De Montfort succeeded in foiling all the Calvinists' attempts against his life. For instance, he would not walk down a certain street at night because something told him that a band of murderers was waiting for him there. Or, when he did find himself at the mercy of one or more cutthroats, he calmly gave them permission to mistreat him *as* they wished—if only they would first promise to mend their evil ways.

"I much prefer the salvation of your soul to ten thousand lives like mine," he told one would-be assassin, smiling. "Go ahead, my friend. Strike!"

These words wrought such terror in the man's heart that he could only stand in trembling silence. Then, after a moment, scarcely able to sheathe a sword, he took to his heels.

"It was terrible!" he told his friends later. "I . . . I couldn't even lift an arm at the look in that priest's eyes! Could it be that he's a good man after all?"

In mid-August of 1711, however, Father De Montfort did fall into an enemy trap. He drank some poisoned soup (served to him after one of his sermons) and for several days was violently ill. Indeed, his life was despaired of, and Brothers Mathurin, John and Nicholas were beside themselves with anxiety. Father De Montfort, only thirty-eight years old, was going to die and leave them all alone!

"What'll we do?" they asked one another in desperation. "We're not priests. We can't give missions by ourselves. . . . "

Father De Montfort reassured them, however, he was very ill—yes. But he would not die. In fact, the approaching mission for soldiers would be a really great success because of this present suffering.

True enough. Little by little Father De Montfort did regain some of his strength, and the mission for soldiers brought the largest crowds of all. When it was over, he even ventured into the country districts to preach to the people there. But in the spring of 1712, when the Bishop of Luçon asked him to go to the Ile d'Yeu, a fishing community some eighteen miles off the coast of Brittany, his many friends urged him to tell the Bishop the truth. He had only partially recovered from the effects of the poisoning and was not really strong enough for missionary work. Besides, the waters surrounding the Ile d'Yeu were infested with British pirates. These men would like nothing better than to put a Catholic priest in chains and carry him off to certain death.

"Nonsense!" exclaimed Father De Montfort. "I'm not sick any more. Just a bit tired once in a while. As for the pirates—I know Our Lady won't let them harm me."

But Father des Bastières (who had helped with the work at Pontchâteau and now had been asked by the Bishop to accompany Father De Montfort on the new missionary venture) was of quite another opinion.

"Father, you don't realize the danger!" he burst out fearfully. "After all, what chance would a little boat like ours have against those swift pirate vessels? Besides, the Governor of the island is a Calvinist and could make things very hard for us."

Father De Montfort laughed. "Good friend, if the holy martyrs had been afraid to suffer for the Faith, they'd not be where they are today," he said cheerfully. "Come on, now. Don't look so sad. Everything's going to be all right."

Poor Father des Bastières! He was a zealous priest, but mortally afraid of dying, and for days he could neither eat nor sleep at the thought of the dangerous trip ahead. Oh, those terrible British pirates! If they didn't torture their captives unmercifully, or put them to death, they generally sold them into slavery in some foreign port. . . .

"It's . . . it's not prudent to go to the Ile d'Yeu," he told himself. "No priest has dared visit there in years. Oh, dear Lord! Please make Father De Montfort explain things to the Bishop and ask for some other assignment!"

But Father De Montfort's mind was made up. The inhabitants of the Ile d'Yeu, of whom there were two thousand or more, had not enjoyed a mission in a long time. Although they had a saintly parish priest, they needed the spiritual tonic that only a mission could supply. Even more. They had never heard of the True Devotion to the Blessed Virgin Mary. Unless they were told about it now, many would die without the extra graces and blessings that could so easily have been theirs.

"We *must* go to those poor people!" he insisted. "They need us, Father."

With a great effort Father des Bastières finally let himself be persuaded. "All right," he muttered. "We probably could do some good on the island." So presently a small fishing boat was hired for the eighteen-mile trip, and on the day appointed Father des Bastières went on board— pale, trembling, and resigned to the worst.

After a few hours, however, his spirits began to rise. The sun was shining, the day pleasant, the wind in the right direction, and not another ship in sight. The boatmen (who had been just as reluctant to make the trip) began to feel better, too. God was blessing the voyage, just as Father De Montfort had promised.

"Nine miles out, and not a sign of the enemy," they told one another, greatly encouraged. "Why, it's almost like a miracle!"

Then suddenly the captain stiffened. What was that looming up on the western horizon—big and black and ominous?

"Not a pirate ship!" he groaned. Then, his eyes straining in their sockets: "Yes, two of them! And coming right for us!"

At once fear filled every heart. After rowing madly for a few minutes, the crew dropped their oars in despair and cowered, trembling, in the bottom of the boat, As for Father des Bastières, he could only stare in hopeless shock at the two black shadows ahead.

"I . . . I knew it!" he muttered through clenched teeth. 'W-we're done for!"

But Father De Montfort, standing in the prow of the little boat, calmly assured his terrified companions that they were under Our Lady's protection and that everything would turn out well.

"Suppose we sing a hymn to our Mother in heaven," he suggested cheerfully.

The captain, as terrified as his men, could scarcely believe his ears. "You surely don't want us to sing now, Father!" he burst out. "Why, the enemy will be on us in less than an hour!'

Father De Montfort nodded. "What of it? Isn't the Blessed Virgin looking after us? Tell the men to start rowing. We're expected on the island, you know, and it wouldn't do to be late."

Reluctantly the crew returned to their oars. But though Father De Montfort began a hymn which everyone knew, his confident voice rang out alone. At such a dreadful moment no one had any heart for singing. Or for anything else. For all realized the truth. No matter what speed their small craft made, it could never hope to escape the gunfire of the fast approaching pirate ships.

"Well, since you won't sing, we'll offer the Rosary instead," said Father De Montfort finally. "That ought to be easy enough. Come on, friends—the Blessed Virgin will protect us, just as I've been telling you."

Half out of their wits with fear, captain and crew joined in the familiar prayer. But try though he would, Father des Bastières could not find his voice. By now the two pirate vessels were in full view, and at any moment the powerful cannons might open fire. . . .

Then suddenly words came to the terrified priest—desperate, high-pitched, pleading: "H-holy Mary, Mother of God . . . p-pray for us sinners . . . now . . . and at the hour of our d-death. . . ."

CHAPTER 35

HOPES FOR THE FUTURE

NEARER and nearer came the pirate vessels, but Father De Montfort scarcely gave them a glance. His worn beads slipped quietly through his fingers as though he were saying his Rosary in some peaceful church. And when the five decades were finished, he calmly announced that the Blessed Virgin had heard their prayer. They were safe.

"S-safe?" stammered Father des Bastières, pointing a shaking finger at the billowing sails of the pirate vessels now only a few hundred yards away. "Just look over there!"

But even as he spoke, there was a gasp of astonishment from captain and crew. The wind had changed! Slowly but surely the two pirate ships were beginning to turn away!

"But . . . but it can't be!" cried one of the men. "Weren't they just getting ready to open fire?"

The captain lowered his spyglass. "Yes," he muttered. "The cannons were trained directly on us. Oh, Father, how did you do it? How did you work a miracle like that?"

Father De Montfort hesitated. "I? Why, I didn't do anything," he said cheerfully. "It was Our Lady who saved us. She often does wonderful things for those who say her Rosary." Then, after a moment: "Perhaps now you feel more like singing a hymn in her honor?"

This time captain and crew were all eagerness, and Father des Bastières joined as earnestly as the rest in the familiar strains of the *Magnificat*.

"Our Lady didn't work this miracle for nothing," he reflected, his heart filled with joyous relief. "We're going to do some wonderful work on the Ile d'Yeu."

True enough. The two-month mission on the little island was a great success, and when it was over Father des Bastières had not the slightest qualm about the return trip to the mainland. In fact, if Father De Montfort had suggested it, he would willingly have set out for wildest Africa. Or for China or Japan. For what real harm could come to anyone who loved and trusted the Mother of God? Who had glimpsed the marvelous power of the Rosary against the forces of evil?

But it was not to foreign lands that duty called Father De Montfort. Upon his arrival in La Rochelle, he began making plans for missions in La Garnache, Sallertaine, Saint-Christophe, Challans and other towns. Then presently he withdrew from public life to give himself to a work that had been in his thoughts for a long time. This was the setting down in writing of the doctrine of the True Devotion to the Blessed Virgin Mary.

Brothers Mathurin, John and Nicholas approved of the new project. It was also a source of satisfaction that recently some friends had purchased a little cottage in Saint-Eloi (a suburb of La Rochelle) and turned it over to their beloved superior.

"He needs a rest from mission work," they told one another. "He'll be able to have it now."

Father De Montfort deeply appreciated the change in occupation—the chance to live as a hermit in his cottage, to pray and think at leisure. But as he set himself to writing about the True Devotion, he also experienced a

Nearer and nearer came the pirate vessels.

certain sadness. The little book he had in mind would do much good—yes. It would inspire in many generous hearts a desire to be the slaves of Jesus in Mary and so win heaven more quickly and easily. But certainly the Devil was not going to stand idly by while all this was taking place. He would sow doubts and misunderstandings where the new book was concerned, just as he had already done with the missions and retreats. For each one who read the book with profit, there would probably be a hundred or more to throw it aside—in bewilderment, in boredom, in downright disagreement. Then there was the depressing premonition that the Evil One would even succeed in having the manuscript lost for several years!

"Still, it'll be found and published some day," he consoled himself. "Our Lady will see to that."

All through the summer and autumn of 1712 Father De Montfort worked on his book. Then in January of 1713 he busied himself with another writing task: that of preparing a Rule for the Company of Mary. True, no priests had yet felt it their vocation to join him in the religious life (not even Father des Bastières), but recently another young man had applied to be a Brother—which brought his present family up to four and made a written Rule something of a necessity.

"Brothers Mathurin, John, Nicholas, Gabriel—all good souls," he reflected as he finished his new task. "But dear Lord! How much longer do I have to wait for priests?" Then, after a moment: "Maybe things would be different if I looked for such helpers in Paris."

Soon he had made up his mind. Yes, he would go to Paris and visit the Seminary of the Holy Ghost, founded by his friend and former classmate, Father Claude des Places. The latter had died four years ago, but perhaps his successor, Father Bouic, would be able to help.

"I'll remind him that Father des Places once promised

me some candidates for the Company of Mary," he decided. "That was a long time ago—back in 1704. But even so, a promise is still a promise. . . . "

In mid-August of that same year, 1713, Father De Montfort arrived in Paris. Father Bouic gave him a warm welcome and lost no time in introducing him to the students of the Seminary. But alas! None of those about to be ordained felt themselves called to missionary life. They preferred to work as parish priests, or to teach. However, four young men who had not yet completed their studies showed some interest in the Company of Mary. Upon Ordination, in two years or so, they would be glad to come to La Rochelle and join the new community.

"You'll certainly be most welcome," said Father De Montfort. "Don't forget. I'll be expecting you."

But as he set about his homeward trip, Father De Montfort's heart was heavy. He was only forty years old, but surely his time on earth was drawing to a close? Despite the variety of medicines supplied by his friends, he had never really recovered from the attempt made by the Calvinists to poison him. Two years had passed since that dreadful day, but the spells of weakness were still with him—the fever, the aches and pains of all sorts.

"I may never live to see those four boys in the Company of Mary," he told himself sadly.

But he quickly banished the discouraging thought. If it was God's Will that his little religious family should prosper, priest-helpers would come. One or two at least. As for Sister Mary Louise. . . .

Anxiety flickered anew in Father De Montfort's eyes. Eight and one-half years had passed since his enemies had driven him from Poitiers, and in all that time Sister Mary Louise had carried on alone at the poorhouse—nursing the sick, keeping the Rule he had written for the Wisdom Group, wearing the habit he had designed, loyally holding to the hope that some day other girls would come to join her in the religious life. Of course there had been letters of direction, and from all accounts she had done wonderful work and had never had to suffer the persecution which he himself had known. Still. . . .

"The poor child has waited long enough," he decided. "I'll go home by way of Poitiers and see if there isn't something I can do to help her." Then, with a little smile: "Maybe I'll visit Catherine Brunet, too. . . ."

CHAPTER 36

SURPRISE FOR SISTER MARY LOUISE

OF course Sister Mary Louise was beside herself with joy when Father De Montfort arrived at the poorhouse. "I . . . I must be dreaming!" she burst out, her eyes bright with happy tears. "The ten years aren't even up yet, and here you are, Father! Oh, how good to see you!"

Father De Montfort smiled at the warm and childlike welcome. And with relief, too. For one shrewd glance had told him that all was well with his spiritual daughter. She was in good health, happy, successful in her work. Indeed, the poorhouse seemed to be thriving as never before—the building and grounds in clean and orderly condition, the staff efficient, the poor themselves well-fed and clothed.

"Child, how did you do it?" he exclaimed incredulously. "Begin at the beginning and tell me everything!"

Sister Mary Louise smiled contentedly as she settled herself for a visit with her spiritual director. Yes, all was well at the poorhouse, she agreed. Of course her mother was still displeased that she was living with the town's outcasts and wearing the grey homespun habit of a Daughter of Wisdom. Then occasionally there were quarrels and misunderstandings among the workers, sickness and death among the poor people. But God had been very good. He had provided many friends and benefactors, so

that when trials did come they did not have to be borne
alone. There was just one big cross. . . .

Father De Montfort nodded understandingly. "I know.
No other girls have come to join you."

"That's right, Father. But of course the ten years aren't
up yet, so I shouldn't complain."

For a moment Father De Montfort was silent. Then he
leaned forward eagerly. "Child, I think someone is coming
to join you very soon," he said.

Sister Mary Louise looked up in astonishment. "Really,
Father? But who?"

"Catherine Brunet."

There was an incredulous pause. Then Sister Mary
Louise shook her head sadly. "Catherine? Oh, no, Father!
She's never wanted to be a nun."

"She does now."

"*What?*"

"Yes, before I came here I had a little visit with her. And
while she didn't actually promise anything, I'm quite sure
that she's finally giving in to God's grace. Mark my words,
she'll be along very soon."

Sister Mary Louise could scarcely believe her ears.
Catherine Brunet, now in her late thirties, who would still
rather sing popular songs than eat, who still had a verita-
ble passion for dancing and pretty clothes—wanted to be
a nun? Surely not! Yet Father De Montfort insisted that
Catherine's worldly ways hid a good heart. She would
make a fine religious.

"After all, child, don't you remember those months when
Catherine lived here with the Wisdom Group? She was
assistant to the blind superior, and did very good work."

Sister Mary Louise nodded slowly. "Yes, Father. I remember. But I remember, too, how she used to laugh and
joke. Why, she even poked fun at you for making a blind
girl superior! She said that was foolish, because any of us

could break the Rule and the blind girl would never know it."

Father De Montfort smiled. "Well, did anyone ever break the Rule?"

"N-no. But on the other hand. . . ."

"What?"

"Oh, Catherine just isn't the type to be a nun, Father! When she was here she was always whistling, even the most sacred hymn tunes. It used to bother me a great deal, although everyone else just laughed about it."

"Whistling hymn tunes isn't a sin."

"Of course not. Still, I can't help feeling that she'll never be happy as a religious."

"Don't worry about that. And don't worry about her lively ways, either. She's the very sort of person who'll endear herself to young people."

At this, Sister Mary Louise turned a bewildered glance upon her spiritual director. *"Young people?* But there aren't any young people here, Father! They're all quite old. In fact, most of them are either bedridden or crippled."

Father De Montfort's heart beat fast. The time had come for him to make known an ambition which, as yet, was shared only with the Bishop and a few close friends in La Rochelle. He had not expected to do more than mention it to Sister Mary Louise on this visit. But now that there had been the successful interview with Catherine Brunet, and probably the Daughters of Wisdom would become a reality very soon. . . .

"Sister, I've a little surprise for you," he said, and proceeded to set forth his cherished plan.

When Catherine came to the poorhouse and asked to be a Daughter of Wisdom, she was to be given the habit and the name of Sister Mary of the Conception. Then for a few months she was to assist Sister Mary Louise. After that they would both come to La Rochelle, where they would occupy themselves with an entirely new work: that of teaching in a free school for girls.

"There's a great need for such a school in La Rochelle, Sister. It's a seaport, you know, and many of the men, being fishermen and sailors, are away from home for months at a time. Families are broken up, children run wild in the streets, and little or nothing is done to help them. The free school for girls will solve many a problem. *And* the one for boys, too—which ought to be opening soon under the direction of some zealous laymen."

Sister Mary Louise listened in silent bewilderment to the unexpected news. She was to leave her beloved poor for a strange work in a strange city? And her companion was to be none other than the high-spirited Catherine Brunet, who had never shown any interest in the religious life?

"Father, I . . . I don't know what to say," she ventured finally. "I've never done any teaching, and neither has Catherine. Our only experience has been here in the poorhouse with the sick and aged."

"Still, both of you can read and write," Father De Montfort reassured her. "And you know the catechism." Then, after a moment: "And you understand about the True Devotion to the Blessed Virgin Mary, too. Oh, Sister! Think what it will mean to explain that to little children!"

Suddenly a new thought came to Sister Mary Louise which served to dispel much of her uncertainty. For more than eight years she had been trying to promote the True Devotion among the inmates of the poorhouse. Results had been good in many cases. But how often she had found only rocky soil for the priceless seed which she had to sow! How often her charges had been too sick or feeble to appreciate the great grace of being totally consecrated to the Blessed Virgin! How often they had died without the consolations of this wonderful gift of God! Whereas if someone had explained matters when they were children. . . .

"You're right, Father!" she agreed enthusiastically. "We ought to do everything possible to make the True Devotion known to young people."

Father De Montfort leaned forward eagerly. "Then you will come to teach in La Rochelle?"

With a courage born of a sudden and very special grace, Sister Mary Louise nodded resolutely. "Yes, Father," she said. "I'll come."

CHAPTER 37

A BROKEN PROMISE

F OR the rest of the day, Father De Montfort was almost
walking on air. What did it matter that he must leave
Poitiers at once, the Bishop (still being under Jansenist
influence) having refused permission for him to offer Mass
anywhere in the diocese? That because of his poor health,
traveling had now become a greater hardship than ever?
Surely nothing mattered, save that the Daughters of
Wisdom were about to become a reality; that countless
children would soon be learning about God and His
Commandments.

"I'm just helping to pay the price," he told himself.
"Dearest Mother, please don't let me spoil things by com-
plaining!"

This thought—that graces are won for others chiefly
through suffering—had been with Father De Montfort
since childhood. Because of it, he had been enabled to
overcome difficulties which would have discouraged the
majority of people. Thus, when an attack of fever forced
him to enter the hospital upon his arrival in La Rochelle,
he was not downcast. Of course he was sick, but he was
still an instrument in God's hands. He was still a missionary, although unable to preach a word. He was still paying
the price for men and women, boys and girls, to appreciate

and practice the True Devotion to the Blessed Virgin Mary.

However, his four lay Brothers were not so resigned. Why, their beloved superior was little more than skin and bones! Surely he would not be with them much longer?

"What'll we do without him?" they asked one another fearfully.

But Father De Montfort was reassuring. No, he would never be completely well again. But he would certainly recover sufficiently to preach several missions. In fact, something told him that he had at least two more years in which to labor for souls.

"That's quite a while, Brothers," he said cheerfully. "We'll be able to do much good in that time."

For several weeks Father De Montfort remained in the hospital. Then, although far from being his old vigorous self, he announced that he was taking up missionary work again. Of course all his friends objected, for it was now wintertime and traveling presented many difficulties even to one who was strong and well.

"It's also the year 1714," replied Father De Montfort, smiling. "Time is growing short. I *must* go!"

When he had done what he could to organize the new free school for boys in La Rochelle, he started forth. Surprisingly enough, his health did not fail and he preached successfully in Courçon, Vanneau and other towns. Then in the spring he gave still more missions, and in June set out for Nantes. He had planned to spend some time here, hoping that the Bishop might now be in a more friendly mood. (The Calvary of Pontchâteau had been destroyed and he himself cleared of every suspicion of being a British spy). But once more his enemies rose up against him, and he left almost immediately for Rennes. Here fresh trials awaited him, too, for he was not allowed to preach.

"Well, since I can't make use of a pulpit, I'll write my friends a letter," he decided. And having made a retreat of several days, he composed his "Letter to the Friends of the Cross," a stirring and heartfelt explanation of the value of suffering.

Despite new persecutions and misunderstandings, Father De Montfort continued with his missionary journeys throughout the balance of the summer and fall. Then, late in November, he returned to La Rochelle. Here news of the best sort awaited him. Three more young men—Philip, James and Louis—wanted to be Brothers in his little community. A letter from Sister Mary Louise informed him that Catherine Brunet had decided to be a religious after all, and was now working with her at the poorhouse as Sister Mary of the Conception. Finally, Bishop de Champflour announced that the free school for boys was flourishing, and that all was in readiness for the opening of the girls' school. All, that is, save the matter of teachers.

"Father, where are those Sisters you told me about?" inquired the Bishop anxiously. "I thought they were coming here to take charge of the work."

Father De Montfort nodded eagerly. "They are, Your Lordship."

"But when?"

"In the spring."

"The spring? But we need them now!"

"Of course. But it'll take a little time for them to wind up affairs in Poitiers. After all, they have to find someone to look after the work at the poorhouse, you know."

The Bishop curbed his impatience as best he could, then suggested that if Father De Montfort felt able, it would be well to arrange for missions in some of the surrounding towns during the coming winter. For instance, there was Fouras—nine miles from La Rochelle; the little island of

Aix; Saint-Laurent-de-la-Prée, Breuil-Magné, and several other parishes. Then in La Rochelle itself the Sisters of Providence were most anxious to have an eight-day retreat.

Father De Montfort promised to do what he could. But as for the Sisters' retreat—well, something told him it ought to be open to all the faithful. The unusual suggestion startled the Bishop, but he finally gave his consent. The retreat would be preached in the public church attached to the convent. And everyone—men, women and children—would be welcome to attend.

It was in early February of 1715 that Father De Montfort returned from his missionary journeys and began preaching to the Sisters. By now he was well-nigh exhausted from his labors. And a bit disappointed, too. For where were the four young men whom he had met at the Seminary of the Holy Ghost in Paris more than two years ago, now ordained priests, who had promised to join him in the religious life, and so make possible the Company of Mary?

"They've changed their minds," he told himself sadly. "They're not coming after all."

It was true. The four had changed their minds in favor of other work. Indeed, one of them—young Father Adrian Vatel—had gone so far as to offer himself for the foreign missions and was even then on his way to India, acting as ship's chaplain in order to pay for his passage. But as luck would have it, his boat put in at La Rochelle during the very week in which Father De Montfort was conducting the retreat for the Sisters of Providence. Learning this, the young priest decided to attend one of the sermons and afterwards to make his apologies to Father De Montfort for having broken his word.

"He'll understand when I explain things," he told himself. "I know he will."

Father De Montfort, worn and tired, was in the act of mounting to the pulpit when Father Vatel entered the church and settled himself expectantly to hear the sermon. But in just a few minutes the latter was experiencing a great disappointment. What was the matter with Father De Montfort? His voice was weak, his words halting, almost as though he had never spoken in public before.

"This can't be the same man who preached so wonderfully at the Seminary in Paris!" he thought. "Why, if he expects to convert people with a talk like this. . . ."

Suddenly Father De Montfort hesitated, then leaned across the pulpit's edge. "There is someone here who is resisting me," he declared, in tones that reached to every corner of the church. "I feel as though the Word of God is lost on him. But he will not get away from me."

Father Vatel sat bolt upright. Surely Father De Montfort didn't mean him! But as the sermon progressed, one doubt after another entered the young priest's mind. Was he doing the right thing in going to the Far East? Were his missionary credentials really in order? Would God bless his work among the pagans? Would his health withstand the hardships of mission life?

"I . . . I shouldn't have come here," he thought, distressed and miserable beyond words. "I'll just slip out quietly and go back to the ship."

But try though he would, he could not bring himself to leave. And presently, the sermon finished, he went in search of Father De Montfort. Once he had planned on just a simple apology for having broken his promise to join the Company of Mary. But now. . . .

"What'll I say?" he asked himself frantically. "What *does* God want of me?"

"Someone here is resisting me!"

CHAPTER 38

THE BARGAIN

IN just a few minutes Father Vatel was more confused
than ever, for Father De Montfort greeted him with an
enthusiasm that was overwhelming.

"Father, at last you've come!" he exclaimed. "God be
praised! What splendid things we'll do together, you and
I!" And he began to describe conditions at Taugonla-
Ronde, the little town where he planned to give his next
mission.

Poor Father Vatel! He did his best to explain that he had
not come to join the Company of Mary but that he was on
his way to India. He had been paid in advance for his services as ship's chaplain, the money spent for books, vestments and other necessities, and in a few hours his ship
would be sailing. He could not possibly stay.

Father De Montfort smiled. "You're not happy about
your new work, though," he observed shrewdly. "Why not,
Father? What's wrong?"

The young priest hesitated. "I . . . I'm happy enough. It's
just that. . . . "

"Your papers aren't in order, perhaps? You doubt that
the Archbishops of Paris and Rouen had the right to send
you to India as a missionary? You feel that such permission should have been obtained from the Pope?"

Father Vatel's eyes shot open with astonishment. "Father! How could you possibly know that?"

"Don't worry. *I know.* And you're right, Father. Your credentials aren't in order. And why? Because God never intended you to work for Him in India. He wants you to stay in France and be my first priest-companion in the Company of Mary."

In vain Father Vatel protested that this was impossible; that he had already spent the money advanced to him and therefore was bound to sail with his ship. Father De Montfort did not seem concerned. Bishop de Champflour would reimburse the ship's owners, and he himself would make things right with the captain.

"Come along, Father," he said. "We haven't any time to lose."

Scarcely knowing what he did, Father Vatel let himself be persuaded. And presently he was experiencing a new and wonderful joy. Gone were the doubts and anxieties of the past several months. For him the future was now assured. He was the first priest to join Father De Montfort's little family! And, poor creature though he was, because of him the Company of Mary had now become a reality!

"I'm not worthy of the privilege," he thought, his heart all but bursting with happiness.

There was little time for idle musing, however. Not only was there the mission at Taugon-la-Ronde to be considered. Arrangements had to be made for the approaching arrival from Poitiers of Sister Mary Louise and Sister Mary of the Conception. The laywomen who were to work with them in the girls' school also needed a few more instructions, and finally there was the question of a mission at Saint-Amand-sur-Sèvre.

Father Vatel plunged into all this work with zest, accompanying Father De Montfort and the Brothers wherever they went—preaching on occasion (although he preferred to leave this duty to his superior), hearing confessions, teaching catechism, organizing religious processions. However, he was not so busy as to forget a special intention which Father De Montfort had recommended to his prayers: namely, that God would soon inspire another priest to join the Company of Mary.

"Who will it be?" he often wondered.

By August of 1715, six months after his own arrival, Sister Mary Louise and Sister Mary of the Conception—now happily settled in La Rochelle—experienced the great joy of being joined in the religious life by two young girls. However, no second priest-helper had come to Father De Montfort, and occasionally Father Vatel found himself just a trifle discouraged.

"Dearest Mother, couldn't you send someone?" he begged.

Then one day in October, while Father De Montfort was preaching to a community of nuns in Fontenay-le-Comte, a young priest arrived with a request that the two members of the Company of Mary come to his brother's parish in Saint-Pompain. It had been many years since a mission had been given there. Surely something could be arranged, even on such short notice?

Father Vatel's heart went out to the newcomer, whose name was Father René Mulot. What a frail young priest he was—paralyzed on one side, suffering from lung trouble, and scarcely able to stand!

"Father, we'd certainly like to come," he said kindly. "But as soon as we leave here, we're scheduled to give a mission in Vouvant. After that, another in Villiers-en-Plaine. Then there's an assignment to Saint-Laurent-sur-Sèvre. Really, I don't see how we could take on any more work just now."

Father René Mulot was suddenly convulsed in a spell of coughing. "I . . . I know you're busy," he said, as soon as he had recovered. "But the people in Saint-Pompain . . . they need a mission so much! Couldn't I at least speak to Father De Montfort about it?"

However, Father De Montfort was of the same opinion as Father Vatel. It would be utterly impossible to go to Saint-Pompain. Besides the many missions that were scheduled for the next few months, the Bishop wanted them to visit La Rochelle in connection with the new free schools. Then Sister Mary Louise needed advice concerning the training of the two girls who had recently joined the Daughters of Wisdom.

"We just couldn't go to your brother's parish, Father," he explained kindly. "There isn't time."

But Father Mulot, weakened by illness though he was, held his ground. How could Father De Montfort refuse this chance to save many souls from hell and make saints of scores of men, women and children in Saint-Pompain?

"Father, you *can't* turn me down!" he gasped. "I've not much longer to live, as you can see. Please, won't you make a dying man happy by granting his one request?"

Father De Montfort hesitated. There was something tremendously appealing about this young priest. Frail though he was, he seemed to have a certain inner strength that told of virtues far beyond the ordinary. Truly, such men were rare.

"Father, I've already told you that we're to open a mission at Vouvant in a few days," he said gently. "That was arranged for long ago. Also the one at Villiers-en-Plaine. But it's just occurred to me that possibly. . . . "

"Yes, Father?"

"We *might* be able to work out something in between for your brother's parish in Saint-Pompain."

Tears glistened in the sick priest's eyes. "Oh, Father!" he burst out. "I . . . I knew you'd understand!"

But Father De Montfort held up his hand in warning. "Wait a minute. I only said we *might* be able to arrange something. It all depends on you."

"On me?"

"Yes." Then, as Father Mulot recovered from another bad coughing spell: "I'll go to your brother's parish on one condition: that you promise to work in the Company of Mary for the rest of your days."

Father Mulot stared in astonishment. "You want *me* to join the Company of Mary?" he whispered incredulously.

"Yes, Father. Rather, it's God Who wants it."

"But . . . but that's impossible! I'm dying!"

"Nothing is impossible with His grace, Father. If you join our group, all your ills will vanish. And you must make your first preaching effort at the mission in Vouvant. Now, what do you say?"

Father Mulot could only sit in numb bewilderment. He, half-paralyzed, afflicted with tuberculosis, asthma and constant headaches was being asked to take up the active life of a missionary and to pledge himself to follow a religious Rule as well? Why, he must be dreaming!

Silently he slumped in his chair, hid his face in his hands and tried to think. There was such great need for a mission in his brother's parish at Saint-Pompain! Scores of men and women there had fallen away from the Church. The True Devotion to the Blessed Virgin Mary was absolutely unknown. And yet. . . .

Presently he roused himself. Everyone knew that Father De Montfort was a saint, that times without number he had worked wonders for sick bodies as well as for sick souls. Then why was he, René Mulot, doubting his word? It could be God's Will that he was meant to be the second priest-member of the Company of Mary; that somehow, in some way, he would be cured of his many ailments. . . .

With pounding heart he struggled to his feet. "All right, Father!" he exclaimed, trembling with excitement and weakness. "I . . . I'll come!"

attendance,
sur-Sèvre, c
hushed and
prayers and
even yet th
would prea(

But on A
was not far
Sacrament:
ciently to si
few posses:
among his
at any mon

The new:
people that
after anoth
ask his ble:

"Give it t

So holdi
the Eleven
De Montfo
moved to te
he began to

But the c
back weak
"H-he's d
But Fatl
Slowly t
evening o
Montfort
glimpsing

CHAPTER 39

THE LAST WORDS OF A SAINT

FATHER Adrian Vatel could scarcely believe his ears when he heard the news, and neither could the Brothers. But when, after a few days of missionary life, their new co-worker was suddenly relieved of his racking cough, the asthma, headaches and all the other pains which had tormented him for years, their amazement knew no bounds.

"Our Father De Montfort is a saint!" they told one another joyfully. "It's his prayers that have cured Father Mulot!"

Yet even as they rejoiced, they watched Father De Montfort with anxiety. If only he could do something for himself! He was so pale and thin, and at times scarcely able to drag himself about. But he only smiled when they begged him to rest and to take things easy. That would hardly be fitting for Our Lady's slave, he said. There was too much work to be done. But in April of the year 1716, when he arrived at Saint-Laurent-sur-Sèvre to give still another mission, Father De Montfort himself came to the realization that his time on earth was about up.

Suddenly a terrible sadness filled his soul. He was forty-three-years-old, and soon he would be called upon to render an account of these years. And what had he to show? A few writings, his missions, the Daughters of Wisdom with four members, the Company of Mary with seven Brothers and two priests.

197

"And I w

Mother, I w

Summon

at Saint-La

fort was to

Bishop de (

to be carrie

Father N

signed to l

themselves

die and the

in La Roch

who were v

"It . . . it

weakly. "I 1

consternat

want you t

kept, that

an increas

Father N

that I'm to

"Yes, tha

"But . . .

health—if

Father I

for you."

Poor Fa

Father De

a certain 1

a saint? A

could he d

ing his wa

Quietly

Five da

beloved su

MARY FABYAN WINDEATT

Mary Fabyan Windeatt could well be called the "storyteller of the saints," for such indeed she was. And she had a singular talent for bringing out doctrinal truths in her stories, so that without even realizing it, young readers would see the Catholic catechism come to life in the lives of the saints.

Mary Fabyan Windeatt wrote at least 21 books for children, plus the text of about 28 Catholic story coloring books. At one time there were over 175,000 copies of her books on the saints in circulation. She contributed a regular "Children's Page" to the monthly Dominican magazine, *The Torch*.

Miss Windeatt began her career of writing for the Catholic press around age 24. After graduating from San Diego State College in 1934, she had gone to New York looking for work in advertising. Not finding any, she sent a story to a Catholic magazine. It was accepted—and she continued to write. Eventually Miss Windeatt wrote for 33 magazines, contributing verse, articles, book reviews and short stories.

Having been born in 1910 in Regina, Saskatchewan, Canada, Mary Fabyan Windeatt received the Licentiate of Music degree from Mount Saint Vincent College in Halifax, Nova Scotia at age 17. With her family she moved to San Diego in that same year, 1927. In 1940 Miss Windeatt received an A.M. degree from Columbia University. Later, she lived with her mother near St. Meinrad's Abbey, St. Meinrad, Indiana. Mary Fabyan Windeatt died on November 20, 1979.

(Much of the above information is from Catholic Authors: Contemporary Biographical Sketches 1930-1947, *ed. by Matthew Hoehn, O.S.B., B.L.S., St. Mary's Abbey, Newark, N.J., 1957.)*